Who's Afraid of
Relativism?

THE CHURCH AND POSTMODERN CULTURE *James K. A. Smith, series editor*
www.churchandpomo.org

The Church and Postmodern
Culture series features high-profile
theorists in continental philosophy
and contemporary theology
writing for a broad, nonspecialist
audience interested in the impact of
postmodern theory on the faith and
practice of the church.

Also available in the series

Who's Afraid of
Relativism?

*Community, Contingency,
and Creaturehood*

James K. A. Smith

Baker Academic
a division of Baker Publishing Group
Grand Rapids, Michigan

Published by Baker Academic
a division of Baker Publishing Group
P.O. Box 6287, Grand Rapids, MI 49516-6287
www.bakeracademic.com

Printed in the United States of America

Library of Congress Cataloging-in-Publication Data
Smith, James K. A., 1970–
    Who's afraid of relativism? : community, contingency, and creaturehood / James K. A. Smith.
        pages cm. — (The church and postmodern culture).
    Includes bibliographical references and index.
    ISBN 978-0-8010-3973-7 (pbk.)
    1. Philosophical theology. 2. Relativity. 3. Pragmatism. 4. Christian philosophy.
5. Wittgenstein, Ludwig, 1889–1951. 6. Rorty, Richard. 7. Brandom, Robert.
    I. Title.
BT40.S656 2014
261.5′1—dc23   2013048241

14 15 16 17 18 19 20   7 6 5 4 3 2 1

If those, however, who are called philosophers happen to have said anything that is true, and agreeable to our faith, the Platonists above all, not only should we not be afraid of them, but we should even claim back for our own use what they have said, as from its unjust possessors.

Augustine

It could all, of course, have been done by the angel; but then no respect would have been shown to our human status, if God appeared to be unwilling to have his word administered to us by other human beings.

Augustine

Now man exists only in dialogue with his neighbor. The infant is brought to consciousness of himself only by love, by the smile of his mother. In that encounter the horizon of all unlimited being opens itself for him, revealing four things to him: (1) that he is one in love with his mother, even in being other than his mother, and therefore all being is one; (2) that that love is good, therefore all being is good; (3) that that love is true, therefore all being is true; and (4) that that love evokes joy, therefore all being is beautiful.

Hans Urs von Balthasar

We should not regret our inability to perform a feat which no one has any idea how to perform.

Richard Rorty

Contents

Series Preface

Current discussions in the church—from emergent "postmodern" congregations to mainline "missional" congregations—are increasingly grappling with philosophical and theoretical questions related to postmodernity. In fact, it could be argued that developments in postmodern theory (especially questions of "post-foundationalist" epistemologies) have contributed to the breakdown of former barriers between evangelical, mainline, and Catholic faith communities. Postliberalism—a related "effect" of postmodernism—has engendered a new, confessional ecumenism wherein we find non-denominational evangelical congregations, mainline Protestant churches, and Catholic parishes all wrestling with the challenges of postmodernism and drawing on the culture of postmodernity as an opportunity for rethinking the shape of our churches.

This context presents an exciting opportunity for contemporary philosophy and critical theory to "hit the ground," so to speak, by allowing high-level work in postmodern theory to serve the church's practice—including all the kinds of congregations and communions noted above. The goal of this series is to bring together high-profile theorists in continental philosophy and contemporary theology to write for a broad, nonspecialist audience interested in the impact of postmodern theory on the faith and practice of the church. Each book in the series will, from different angles and with different questions, undertake to answer questions such as, What does postmodern theory have to say about the shape of the church? How should concrete, in-the-pew and on-the-ground religious practices be impacted by postmodernism? What should the church look like in postmodernity? What has Paris to do with Jerusalem?

The series is ecumenical not only with respect to its ecclesial destinations but also with respect to the facets of continental philosophy and theory that are represented. A wide variety of theoretical commitments will be included, ranging from deconstruction to Radical Orthodoxy, including voices from Badiou to Žižek and the usual suspects in between (Nietzsche, Heidegger, Levinas, Derrida, Foucault, Irigaray, Rorty, and others). Insofar as postmodernism occasions a retrieval of ancient sources, these contemporary sources will be brought into dialogue with Augustine, Irenaeus, Aquinas, and other resources. Drawing on the wisdom of established scholars in the field, the series will provide accessible introductions to postmodern thought with the specific aim of exploring its impact on ecclesial practice. The books are offered, one might say, as French lessons for the church.

Preface

Like the title of Jussi Adler-Olsen's crime novel, I sometimes feel like "the keeper of lost causes," the patron of bad ideas. I have a habit of affirming what other Christians despise (and vice versa!). I tend to be nonplussed by the supposed resources offered to Christian thought by "mainstream" philosophy, which puts me on the outs with most trends in contemporary Christian philosophy (e.g., evidentialist apologetics or "analytic theology"). Instead, I try to give a fair hearing to schools of thought that seem not only unhelpful to Christian understanding but downright inhospitable and antithetical—often only to discover that the script is flipped and these "godless" philosophers might actually have something to teach us. Even more strongly, their work might be a catalyst for us to remember aspects of Christian orthodoxy that we have forgotten—a forgetting that sometimes happens in the name of defending orthodoxy.

In *Who's Afraid of Postmodernism?* I took up the unholy trinity of Jacques Derrida, Jean-François Lyotard, and Michel Foucault as allies in the task of formulating a "catholic" postmodernism. Rather than seeing them primarily as threats or "defeaters" of the faith, I explored the ways that their philosophical critique of modernity was a catalyst for the church to remember what it had forgotten. I did so in the Augustinian spirit of "looting the Egyptians"—stealing philosophical insights from the pagans and putting them to service in worship of the Triune God, hoping

11

to avoid melting them down into golden calves. This strategy of bringing "every thought captive" to Christ has long marked Christian engagement with philosophy. I just exported it from Greece to France.

I see this book as an extension of that project, now staging a heist of the pragmatists Ludwig Wittgenstein, Richard Rorty, and Robert Brandom to help us grapple with a phenomenon often associated with postmodernity: relativism. But once again, I'm staking out a position that is not likely to be popular, or will at least seem counterintuitive, if not downright dangerous. My thesis is that Christians *should* be "relativists," of a sort, precisely because of the biblical understanding of creation and creaturehood. I leave it to the remainder of this book to actually try to make a case for that intuition, and to tease out its implications (which might not be what you think they are).

Engaging pragmatism is also a belated demand for me. It is a philosophical tradition that points out some of the problems with French phenomenology, which has shaped my thinking hitherto. In many ways, I was prompted to finally undertake this line of research because of the exemplary work of Charles Taylor, who has been my philosophical north star over the last several years.

While this book has a constructive project of advancing a "Christian pragmatism" and exploring the implications of that for theology and ministry, I also hope it can serve a pedagogical purpose as an accessible introduction to an important philosophical tradition and three key philosophers whose works are notoriously difficult and slippery. Much of the book simply offers a clear exposition of these philosophers and a representative text from each: Ludwig Wittgenstein's *Philosophical Investigations* (1953), Richard Rorty's *Philosophy and the Mirror of Nature* (1979), and Robert Brandom's concise work *Articulating Reasons* (2000). Together, these comprise an ongoing conversation in the late twentieth century that continues to reverberate in the twenty-first. In a way, this book should be read alongside these primary texts; but it might also be that this book could first be read as a portal to these challenging primary works. Some more technical points are pushed down into footnotes so that undergraduate students need not be distracted by more arcane issues. But graduate and seminary students, as well as scholars, will want to look carefully at the qualifications and extensions suggested in the notes. In order to try to illustrate key philosophical concepts and to help students "picture" the issues under discussion, each of the first four chapters includes expositions of a film: *Wendy and Lucy* (chap. 1), *Lars and the Real Girl* (chap. 2), *Crazy Heart* (chap. 3), and *I've Loved You So Long* (chap. 4). Just as readers would do well to have the primary texts alongside this book, so too I hope readers might watch these films as artistic parallels to my argument. I hope those professors who use the book as a textbook might find ways to incorporate the films into their pedagogy.

This book is best understood as an essay: a focused, idiosyncratic angle on some themes and issues. There are, no doubt, vast literatures that could have been consulted that don't appear in the footnotes. I make no claims to have "mastered" the field in this regard. This is but a foray. My task is exploratory and programmatic, not exhaustive and pedantic. The book simply grows out of first-hand encounter with primary texts, discussed with students over the past several years, with a view to addressing a challenge often bandied about at youth retreats: the specter of relativism. The orienting conviction is that if, even on a "popular" level, we are going to invoke philosophical concepts—even if only as philosophical bogeymen—we have some responsibility to make ourselves accountable to philosophy. So think of this little book as an exercise in philosophical accountability.

The core of this book was worked out in two renditions of my senior philosophy seminar, Philosophy of Language and Interpretation. I'm profoundly grateful to the students at Calvin College—both philosophy majors and not—who are willing to sit around that seminar table, prepared and eager to discuss difficult texts and grapple with disconcerting questions, all while tolerating my ridiculously muddled "diagrams" that are *intended* to make things clear. I have learned much from them, and this book is in many ways a fruit of teacher-student collaboration.

I also enjoyed the opportunity to crystallize a first draft of several chapters when I was invited to give the 2013 H. Orton Wiley Lectures at Point Loma Nazarene University in San Diego, California. I'm grateful to Professor Brad Kelle, Provost Kerry Fulcher, and the entire PLNU community for their hospitality and gracious reception of the lectures. Conversations there helped me hone points of the argument. Turning those lectures into a book was made possible by the generous sabbatical afforded me by Calvin College in the spring of 2013. I then received helpful critical feedback on the manuscript from Ron Kuipers, Chad Lakies, and Tommy Graves, to whom I'm grateful.

The completion of this book was not without its challenges. And like so many authors, I wish I had more time to let it percolate, ripen, mature—pick your metaphor. But then I was reminded of Wittgenstein's comment in a 1945 preface to the book that would be published as the *Philosophical Investigations*: "I should have liked to produce a good book. This has not come about, but the time is past in which I could improve it."[1] It seemed fitting that a book that argues for a Christian appreciation of contingency, finitude, and dependence should be sent off into the world with some fear and trembling, but also hope and trust.

---

1. Ludwig Wittgenstein, *Philosophical Investigations*, 3rd ed., trans. G. E. M. Anscombe (New York: Macmillan, 1953), vi.

1

"It Depends"

Creation, Contingency, and the Specter of Relativism

The Specter of Relativism

If there is any clear and present danger in our postmodern world, surely it is "relativism." Identified as the enemy by everyone from youth pastors to university presidents, relativism is both a universal threat and common rallying cry. It is the monster that will make away with our children while at the same time eroding the very foundations of American society (apparently relativism is going to be very busy!).

In fact, for some Christian commentators, postmodernism just *is* relativism. J. P. Moreland, for example, claims that postmodernism "represents a form of cultural relativism about such things as reality, truth, reason, value, linguistic meaning, the self and other notions. On a postmodern view, there is no such thing as objective reality, truth, value, reason, and so forth. All these are social constructions, creations of linguistic practices, and as such are relative not to individuals but to social groups that share a narrative."[1] In

---

1. J. P. Moreland, *Kingdom Triangle: Recover the Christian Mind, Renovate the Soul, Restore the Spirit's Power* (Grand Rapids: Zondervan, 2007), 77.

a similar vein, D. A. Carson shares Moreland's worry and succinctly assesses the situation: "From the perspective of the Bible,"
he concludes, "relativism is treason against God and his word."[2]

This isn't just an evangelical worry either. In a homily just before the conclave that elected him pope, Joseph Ratzinger decried
what he described as the "dictatorship of relativism": "Today," he
noted, "having a clear faith based on the Creed of the Church is
often labeled as fundamentalism. Whereas relativism, that is, letting oneself be 'tossed here and there, carried about by every wind
of doctrine,' seems the only attitude that can cope with modern
times. We are building a dictatorship of relativism that does not
recognize anything as definitive and whose ultimate goal consists
solely of one's own ego and desires."[3]

We seem to have an ecumenical consensus here: relativism is
the very antithesis of the "absolute truth" (Absolute Truth) we
proclaim in the gospel. Relativism is something we should be worried about, even afraid of. So who in their right mind would sign
up to defend such a monster?

Well, I'd like to give it a shot. Or, at least, I would like to
introduce some nuance into our reactionary dismissals and cari-
catured fear-mongering—particularly because I'm concerned
with what is offered as an antidote: claims to "absolute" truth.
In some ways, the medicine might be worse for faith than the
disease. Should we be afraid of relativism? Perhaps. But should
we be equally afraid of the "absolutism" that is trotted out as
a defense? I think so. And not because it violates the dictates of
liberal toleration, but because it harbors a theological impulse
that might just be heretical. The Christian *re*action to relativism
betrays a kind of theological tic that characterizes contemporary
North American Christianity—namely, an evasion of contingency
and a suppression of creaturehood. In this respect, I think "postmodern relativism" (a term that would only ever be uttered by
critics, with a dripping sneer) often appreciates aspects of our
finite creaturehood better than the Christian defenses that seem
to inflate our creaturehood to Creator-hood. In other words, I

2. D. A. Carson, *The Intolerance of Tolerance* (Grand Rapids: Eerdmans, 2012),
132.
3. Joseph Cardinal Ratzinger, Mass for the Election of the Supreme Pontiff, St. Peter's Basilica, April 18, 2005, http://www.ewtn.com/pope/words/conclave_homily.asp.

think relativists might have something to teach us about what it means to be a *creature*.

But "relativism" is a pretty hazy figure, and there is nothing like a unified "school" of "relativist thought" (despite how some critics might talk).[4] So to focus our target, and thus avoid throwing misguided haymakers at a vague sparring partner, I'm going to consider a specific case: the philosophical school of thought described as "pragmatism." My reasoning is simple: whenever critics begin to decry "postmodern relativism" (say it out loud, with a gravelly scowl), inevitably we know whose name is going to come up: Richard Rorty, whipping boy of middlebrow Christian intellectuals and analytic philosophers everywhere, the byword for everything that is wrong with postmodernism and academia. The Rorty scare is like the red menace, giving license to philosophical McCarthyism and rallying the troops in defense.

Now, I think many of these critics *should* be worried by Rorty. He calls into question some of our most cherished shibboleths and clichés, pulling out the rug from beneath some of our most fundamental philosophical assumptions. I'm not out to show that Rorty is no threat, nor is my goal to disclose the "real" Rorty who will turn out to be a tame friend of the philosophical status quo. To the contrary, Rorty's pragmatism *does* have all the features of the "relativism" Christians love to castigate and fume against. That's why, when Christian scholars are looking for a foil, Rorty inevitably appears.

However, I also think it is important to situate Rorty within a philosophical lineage—and that lineage is what he describes as "pragmatism," a school of thought he (rather idiosyncratically) saw stemming from the triumvirate of Ludwig Wittgenstein, John Dewey, and Martin Heidegger.[5] We might think of pragmatism as postmodernism with an American accent: a little more

4. If anyone uses the plural noun "postmoderns" to describe a group of people, you can be pretty confident that person is working with a caricature.

5. Later pragmatists like Robert Brandom and Jeffrey Stout see the heritage as even older, going back to Hegel—not the Hegel of the *Phenomenology of Spirit* but more the *ethical* Hegel—the Hegel of *Elements of a Philosophy of Right*. See, for example, Robert Brandom's invocations of Hegel in his afterword to *Between Saying and Doing* (Oxford: Oxford University Press, 2008), 216–17. But Rorty also tips his hat to Hegel in *Philosophy and the Mirror of Nature* (Princeton: Princeton University Press, 1979), 135.

straightforward and a little less mercurial than French theory, but still a radical critique of the modern philosophical project.[6] Inspired by the later Wittgenstein of the *Philosophical Investigations*, Rorty's *Philosophy and the Mirror of Nature* is a stark but serious articulation of "relativism."[7] And the work of Rorty's student Robert Brandom has extended this "pragmatist" project even while also offering a critique of both Wittgenstein and Rorty.

So if we want to take relativism seriously, we can't rail against a chimera of our own making, congratulating ourselves for having knocked down a straw man. To avoid this, I'm suggesting that we engage this pragmatist stream in Anglo-American philosophy as a serious articulation of "relativism." This will make us accountable to a body of literature and not let us get away with vague caricatures. So my procedure is to offer substantive expositions of works by Wittgenstein, Rorty, and Brandom, which are not often provided by their critics who love to pluck quotes out of context in order to scandalize (or terrify) the masses. We will see how their arguments unfold, why they reach the conclusions they do, and *then* assess how we ought to think about it all from a Christian perspective. As I've already hinted, I actually think there is something for us to learn from these philosophers—that pragmatism can be a catalyst for Christians to remember theological convictions that we have forgotten in modernity. Granted, none of these pragmatists have any interest in defending orthodox Christianity; I won't pretend otherwise. But I will suggest that taking them seriously might actually be an impetus for us to recover a more orthodox Christian faith—a faith more catholic than the modernist faith of their evangelical despisers.

Let me clarify from the outset: I can pretty much guarantee I'm one of the most conservative people in the room, so to speak. So please don't think I'm trotting this out as a prelude to offering you a "progressive" Christianity. Indeed, I will argue that if pragmatism helps us understand the conditions of finitude, then our trajectory should be "catholic."[8] The end of my project is not an eviscerated, liberal Christianity but, in fact, a catholic conservatism.

6. Cf. Nancey Murphy, *Anglo-American Postmodernity: Philosophical Perspectives on Science, Religion, and Ethics* (Boulder, CO: Westview, 1997).

7. Rorty is even more explicit about this in *Objectivity, Relativism, and Truth* (Cambridge: Cambridge University Press, 1990).

8. In this sense, my argument here parallels the conclusions I reached (via different channels) in *Who's Afraid of Postmodernism?*

The Kids Are Not All Right: Relativism, Social Constructionism, and Anti-Realism

In order to motivate our immersion in Wittgenstein, Rorty, and Brandom, I would like to try to concretize this "specter" of relativism a bit more seriously—though that's a bit like trying to catch a ghost. To do so, I will engage two sober, scholarly critics of relativism: sociologist Christian Smith and philosopher Alvin Plantinga. Both exemplary Christian scholars, they share a common critique of the bogeyman of postmodernism as a form of relativism. So rather than trotting out easy targets that could be easily dismissed, I want you to hear critiques of relativism characterized by both scholarly rigor and Christian concern.

Christian Smith on Social Constructionism

Relativism traffics under other names and mutates into different forms. One of those is "social constructionism" (or "constructivism"): the notion that we somehow *make* our world. Rather than being a collection of brute facts that we bump up against, social constructionism emphasizes that "the world" is an environment of our making. So rather than being accountable to a "real" world that imposes itself on our concepts and categories, in fact our concepts *create* "reality." Christian Smith is concerned with its strongest[9] form, which claims something like the following:

9. Smith distinguishes between what he calls "weak" social constructionism and "strong" social constructionism in *What Is a Person? Rethinking Humanity, Social Life, and the Moral Good from the Person Up* (Chicago: University of Chicago Press, 2010), 121–22. He actually affirms "weak" social constructionism (he calls it a "realist" version of the claim) as simply recognizing that "all human knowledge is conceptually mediated and can be and usually is influenced by particular and contingent sociocultural factors such as material interests, group structures, linguistic categories, technological development, and the like—such that what people believe to be real is significantly shaped not only by objective reality but also by their sociocultural contexts" (122). It is tempting to deflect his critique of postmodernism by showing that folks like Rorty hold to something like this. But I won't do so. I think Smith is right to hear in Rorty something more radical, closer to what he calls "strong" social constructionism. However, below I will suggest that this weak/strong distinction is very unstable and ultimately untenable.

> Reality itself for humans is a human, social construction, con-
> stituted by human mental categories, discursive practices, defini-
> tions of situations, and symbolic exchanges that are sustained as
> "real" through ongoing social interactions that are in turn shaped
> by particular interests, perspectives, and, usually, imbalances of
> power—our knowledge about reality is therefore entirely culturally
> relative, since no human has access to reality "as it really is" . . .
> because we can never escape our human epistemological and lin-
> guistic limits to verify whether our beliefs about reality correspond
> with externally objective reality.[10]

Now that *does* sound like something to be worried about. Social constructionism, you might say, is the scholarly rendition of
relativism that Smith sets out to critique. Notice its features: it
begins with the assumption that humans *constitute* our "reality";
that this act of "making" our world is inevitably *social* and thus
depends on a community or society or "people"; that our knowledge of reality is therefore *relative to* the categories and concepts
that our community gives us; and that this means we can never
"know" whether our beliefs *correspond* to reality because there
would be no way to step outside a community to check whether
our categories "match" an *external* reality.

In this description you can also hear Smith's worry: if social
constructionism were true, then there are no checks and balances,
no "outside" that could curb our inventions and preferences. We
could just make up the world any old way we want—and if "we"
want horrible things or want to create a "reality" in which slavery
or racism or pedophilia are "good," there's nothing to stop us. This
is why the specter of relativism becomes scariest when we get to
morality: rather than being a vague, almost trivial puzzlement about
mundane matters ("You mean some people don't think there really
are pelicans outside of my cranium?!"), things start to get serious,
and scary, when we start talking about moral issues ("You mean
some people think we can just make up our own morality—that
there's no right or wrong?!").

Smith's account gets there soon enough. If social constructionism is true, he concludes, then there are no "objective" moral facts

---

10. Ibid., 122. (And yes: that was one sentence in the original!)

or standards "outside" of us and our communities.[11] And if that's the case, then "anything goes."[12]

You can see where this is going. If our moral categories are nothing more than the expressions of some community's preferences, then there will be no recourse to critique a *bad* community's bad morals. So, for example, "racism and injustice are indexed as morally wrong for us. But what if some other person or community constructively 'indexes' the social patterns behind those 'wrongs' as morally acceptable—as some in fact do? The constructionist, by virtue of the innate intellectual limitations of his or her own theoretical system, has no more persuasive leverage to apply."[13] Constructionism and relativism seem to leave us in the position of being unable to prevent racism, oppression, and other forms of injustice because they can't avail themselves of moral "facts." "All that is in fact left in this approach for the making of moral

11. Smith actually trots out the "self-defeating" critique at this point—that strong constructionism is morally self-defeating because most social constructionists actually have very strong views about what a *better* society looks like; but to advocate for a *better* society "presumes the possession of real moral standards" (ibid., 138); yet of course it is just such moral standards that strong constructionism eradicates "by denying the existence of real moral facts" (139). So Smith effectively says to the constructionist/relativist: you can't have your cake and eat it too. But there is another option—namely, an account of how one could have *moral* standards without having to claim that they are "objective." As we'll see, this is precisely what Rorty hopes to offer. (We'll have to see whether his account is adequate.)

Finally, Smith has a bit of a habit of assuming what he's supposed to be proving: so social constructionism is taken to be wrong *because* it precludes "real moral facts" (139)—even "real moral standards" (138). But that's not an *argument* against social constructionism. You can't say social constructionism is wrong *because* it doesn't get you what "moral realism" does, since the difference between them is precisely what's at issue. We'll return to this below.

12. Consider, for example, how Smith defines "moral relativism" elsewhere.

By "moral relativism" we mean the descriptive belief that moral standards are culturally defined—that the truth or falsity of moral claims and judgments is not universal or objective but instead relative to the particular historical and cultural beliefs, views, traditions, and practices of particular groups of people, which leads to the normative belief that everyone ought to tolerate all of the moral beliefs and belief-justified behaviors of others, even when they are very different from our own cultural or moral standards, since no universal or objective moral standard exists by which to judge their beliefs and behaviors. (*Souls in Transition: The Dark Side of Emerging Adulthood* [New York: Oxford University Press, 2011], 251n4)

13. Smith, *What Is a Person?*, 140.

commitments are personal preference, arbitrary choice, and power to enforce and impose."[14]

It is in this context that Smith makes his pitch for "moral realism" as an antidote to the relativism of (strong) social constructionism.[15] But one might ask whether he immediately overreaches, since he puts it this way: "It is *only* a belief in the existence of truths that are independent of our thinking about them that can motivate the desire to subjugate our desires, preferences, ideologies, and politics to the search for truth as best as we can grasp it."[16] Only a "realism" that accounts for our beliefs as "corresponding" to an "objective" reality can really be *moral*. Smith continues: "The fact that for most of us the world is not the way we would like it to be tells us that a largely objective reality exists that powerfully affects our lives, which is much more than simply the product of human interactions. If so, then our knowledge of that reality should be shaped as much as possible by the objective nature of its being, not by our projected desires and preferences for it. That is realism."[17]

It's the *"only"* that is the problem here. First, Smith's claim is largely stipulative and unwarranted—asserted as if it were just "obvious," but not demonstrated. But second, it just seems empirically false.[18] For example, Richard Rorty is very much committed to the amelioration of suffering, and *motivated* to change the shape of our society; indeed, he's a veritable evangelist for democracy. But he has this desire and motivation *without* the "realist" ontology that Smith says is a *requirement* for such reform. For Smith to retort

14. Ibid., 141.

15. In addition to the question raised below, this raises another question: If relativist constructionism is a relatively new phenomenon, displacing age-old "realism" and the tradition of "moral absolutes," then isn't it fair to ask, How did good old traditional realism fare in preventing racism and injustice? Indeed, what do we make of those racists who are realists—who are confident that they see things "the way they are," who believe that their conceptual categories correspond to "reality?" What of those who take it as a "moral fact" that whites are the superior race? It seems that realism might not be much of a pragmatic or moral advantage in this respect.

16. Ibid., 143–44, emphasis added.

17. Ibid., 145. Yes, "that" is realism; but "realism" includes some epistemological and ontological commitments *beyond* what's just been stated. As I will show in chap. 3, Rorty can affirm almost everything Smith says here, but wouldn't thereby commit himself to "realism."

18. I use the term "false" knowing that Smith might object, but as we'll see later, realists are not the only ones who can avail themselves of the terms "true" and "false."

that Rorty is trapped by incoherence is not very persuasive; Rorty is a pretty smart guy, and he's heard this before, so maybe—just maybe—there's more to this?

Here we get to one of my core concerns in this book. The "realism" that Smith invokes and defends is not just an ethical theory. It is ultimately rooted in a metaphysics and a philosophy of language. Smith himself recognizes that what's at issue here is a *philosophical* question "of the relation among language, reality, and knowledge."[19] In other words, we're bumping up against fundamental issues in philosophy of language—and Smith concedes that he's no philosopher of language.[20] Nor does he consult philosophers of language or school himself on the state of the question in their field. So what we get is a bit of freelance philosophizing by a sociologist, making quite grand claims about the need to recover a "referential theory of language" and a "correspondence" theory of truth, with nary attention to the *philosophical* challenges to such a theory over the past fifty years.

Now I'm the last person to decry interdisciplinary efforts. So I am not criticizing Smith for traipsing on the turf of philosophers. He's absolutely right: the questions posed by social constructionism in the social sciences lead to fundamental issues in philosophy of language and metaphysics—questions of how we understand the relation between language and reality. I applaud him for recognizing this and tackling the issues. But our interdisciplinary forays need to make themselves accountable to the state of the conversation in those relevant fields, and it's here that I find Smith's account lacking. While this book will amount to a critique of his proposal, I hope it might also be viewed as something of an assist: a philosopher of language taking up the issues that Smith has rightly raised.

And this is where the pragmatism of Wittgenstein, Rorty, and Brandom is directly relevant. In fact, I agree with much of Smith's critique of the incoherence of "strong" constructionism, which really just ends in skepticism.[21] But I think there is a form of

19. Smith, *What Is a Person?*, 154.
20. Ibid., 159.
21. Smith focuses on the incoherence of many forms of strong constructionism by noting that most proposals stem from an acceptance of Ferdinand de Saussure's theory of language (*What Is a Person?*, 153–57). I think Smith is right to point out incoherencies in this school of thought, which retains the basic shape of a "representationalist" epistemology but then denies any role for a "referent." Indeed, I think the

constructionism (you might even say "relativism") that Smith has
not actually addressed—a form that stems from Wittgenstein and
is characteristic of the philosophical tradition known as "pragmatism." The only social constructionism that will be able to evade
Smith's critique will be a pragmatist version that emerges from
Wittgenstein's more radical critique of *representationalism* (or
referentialism). These are roughly synonymous ways of describing
a particular view of the relationship between language, reality, and
knowledge as a relation of ideas ("representations") in my mind
that "correspond" to reality "outside" my mind. Charles Taylor,
commenting on Wittgenstein's critique, calls this the inside/outside
picture of knowledge (the "I/O picture," for short): knowledge is
a matter of getting something "inside" our minds to hook onto
things "outside" our minds.[22]

But for pragmatists like Wittgenstein, Rorty, and Brandom, this
"picture" is precisely the problem. "A *picture* held us captive,"
Wittgenstein remarked in the *Investigations*. "And we could not
get outside it, for it lay in our language and language seemed to
repeat it to us inexorably."[23] "Realism" of the sort Christian Smith
is touting is the answer to a question we shouldn't be asking,
precisely because it is predicated on this I/O picture. And this I/O
representationalist picture has even become sedimented into our
"folk" epistemologies, our everyday assumptions about how we
relate to the world. Because the I/O picture has settled into our

---

work of Jacques Derrida (who has been influential for some of my own earlier work)
remains captive to a "picture" here that is precisely the problem—which is why some
forms of deconstruction never quite escape a representationalist paradigm and end up
as a kind of skepticism. But as I will show, following Charles Taylor, there is a more
radical stream of social constructionism that rejects this whole representationalist
"picture" of knowledge and beliefs.

22. Charles Taylor, "Merleau-Ponty and the Epistemological Picture," in *The Cambridge Companion to Merleau-Ponty*, ed. Taylor Carman and Mark B. N. Hansen
(Cambridge: Cambridge University Press, 2005), 26. In a related article, Taylor points
out that this epistemological picture is mechanistic: "If we see [perception] as another
process in a mechanistic universe, we have to construe it as involving as a crucial com-
ponent the passive reception of impressions from the external world. Knowledge then
hangs on a certain relation holding between what is 'out there' and certain inner states
that this external reality causes in us." Taylor, "Overcoming Epistemology," in *Philosophical Arguments* (Cambridge, MA: Harvard University Press, 1995), 3–4. This is why,
below, we'll often find Rorty and Brandom talking about thermostats and photocells.

23. Ludwig Wittgenstein, *Philosophical Investigations*, 3rd ed., trans. G. E. M.
Anscombe (New York: Macmillan, 1953), §115.

"everyday" attitude, it is "natural" for us to have "realist" worries. Indeed, the picture fools us into thinking that if we reject correspondence or representationalism, we're rejecting reality. And it is very hard to break out of this picture. As Taylor comments, "It is not enough to escape its activity just to declare that one has changed one's opinion on these questions. One may, for instance, repudiate the idea of representation, claim that one has no truck with this, that nothing lies between us and the world we know, and still be laboring within the picture."[24]

This is precisely the situation when it comes to Christian Smith's attempt to revive realism, albeit a "critical" realism. More critically, Smith's rather naïve invocation of the need to recover a "referentialist" account of language seems blithely unaware of the force and features of the pragmatist critique of reference and representation.[25] The only relativism worth its salt—the only relativism worth engaging, and from which we might have something to learn—will be a relativism that calls into question this picture—calls into question just the referentialism that Smith extols.[26] But does that mean that *truth* is called into question? Or that core claims of the Christian faith are eviscerated? Is "realism" the only way to affirm something as *true*? I don't think so, and it is the hasty assumption otherwise that I want to contest in this book.

Alvin Plantinga on Anti-realism

I've suggested that relativism wears many masks. At times it shows up as sophomoric, popular renditions like, "Well, that might

24. Taylor, "Overcoming Epistemology," 28. Taylor goes on to consider how this picture remains operative in the work of Donald Davidson, even though Davidson is a radical critic of "foundationalism" (28–30).

25. Taylor goes on to explain how it is representationalism and the I/O picture, not pragmatism, that leads to skepticism (ibid., 38–39).

26. This is why, ultimately, the distinction between "weak" and "strong" social constructionism is irrelevant. "Weak" social constructionism—or Smith's "critical realism"—is still *referentialist* and *representationalist*, continuing to accept the "inside/outside" anthropology that undergirds this epistemology (Taylor). It is this picture that pragmatism calls into question, and I suggest that (1) nothing about Christian faith *requires* that we accept representationalism, and (2) there might be good theological reasons to reject such a representationalism and thus agree with the pragmatists—to a point. Rorty would say that critical realism is the answer to a question we should stop asking.

be wrong for you, but not for me." There are also more sophisti-
cated forms, as we saw in social constructionist accounts of reality.
Another scholarly or "academic" form of relativism traffics under
the banner of "anti-realism."[27] As you might guess, anti-realism
is "against"—or at least denies—just the sort of "realism" that
Christian Smith defends. But while realists hastily surmise that this
means anti-realists deny the existence of an extra-cranial world,
in fact what these so-called anti-realists are usually denying is the
representationalist picture of knowledge that posits an inside/out-
side. In that sense, pragmatists like Rorty are not "anti-realists"
because they think the whole realist/anti-realist debate rests on
a category mistake—a contingent, faulty, "modern" picture of
knowledge that we should reject.

As you can imagine, it's not a far distance from *moral* worries about relativism (or anti-realism) to specifically *theological*
worries. If relativism obliterates moral facts, what does it do
to God? In its strongest form, the worry about social constructionism would be that it means *we* "construct" God—that God,
rather than being an eternal, transcendent Being who precedes
us (and speaks to us, and loves us), is instead a product of our
social construction, an invention we create. There "is" no "God"
apart from the entity/concept that we "construct." In Feuerbach's
version of this deflationary account of religious belief, God is
actually *us* writ large, a projection of all that we are not.[28] If *that*
is the implication of relativism, then it is clearly a view antithetical to orthodox Christian faith. So we need to grapple with this
challenge.

Alvin Plantinga deals with such accounts as possible "defeaters"
of Christian belief.[29] And he explicitly addresses Rorty's deflation-

27. See Alvin Plantinga, "How to Be an Anti-Realist," presidential address to the
Western Division of the APA, April 29, 1982, in *Proceedings and Addresses of the
American Philosophical Association* 56 (1982): 47–70. Plantinga targets the "Conti-
nental Anti-Realism in such philosophers as Richard Rorty" and the "Linguistic Anti-
Realism of Wittgenstein and his many followers" in his Stob Lectures, *The Twin Pillars
of Christian Scholarship*, in *Seeking Understanding: The Stob Lectures, 1986–1998*
(Grand Rapids: Eerdmans, 2001), 128–32.

28. See Ludwig Feuerbach, *The Essence of Christianity*. For sympathetic discussion, see Van A. Harvey, *Feuerbach and the Interpretation of Religion* (Cambridge:
Cambridge University Press, 1997).

29. See Plantinga's explanation of "defeaters" (and defeater defeaters) in *Warranted
Christian Belief* (New York: Oxford University Press, 2000), 359–66.

ary account of truth as an example of a potential "postmodern" defeater, asking quite simply, "Is postmodernism inconsistent with Christian belief?" The beginning of Plantinga's answer is worth noting. In some ways, he says, "postmodern" claims are not defeaters of Christian belief because "some of them are entirely congenial to it. For example, postmoderns typically reject classical foundationalism, which has also been rejected by such doughty spokespersons for Christian belief as Abraham Kuyper, William Alston, and Nicholas Wolterstorff and, for that matter, in an anticipatory fashion by Augustine, Aquinas, Calvin, and Edwards."[30] So you heard it from Plantinga first: Kuyper and Rorty might not be as far apart as one might think.

But let's not sit down for a round of "Kumbaya" just yet. "Other postmodern claims," Plantinga emphasizes, "do appear to be incompatible with Christian belief: for example, the claims that God is dead, that there are no 'objective' moral standards, and perhaps also the claim that there isn't any such thing as *truth*, at least as commonsensically thought of."[31]

I haven't run into many so-called "postmodern" theorists who actually go around saying "there isn't any such thing as *truth*." That would be a bit too earnest and direct, not befitting their irony. It's certainly not something that Rorty says. Instead of seeing them reject "any such thing as truth," it would be better to say that they offer us *deflationary accounts* of truth. They *explain* truth in terms other than our (realist) habits incline us to. So they don't deny truth, nor do they forfeit the ability to be able to say, "X is true"; they just don't think that truth is a mechanism by which concepts in our heads magically hook onto entities outside of our heads. If *that* is how you usually think about truth—if that is your default and "commonsensical" picture of truth—then it will seem like Rorty is denying that there is truth. But in fact he's just not buying the story we usually tell about truth.

30. Ibid., 423. He goes on to note that postmodernism and Christianity share concerns about the poor, oppression, and systemic injustice, and both have a hearty sense of self-suspicion and hold to fallibilism (424).

31. Ibid., 424, his emphasis. Both Rorty and Charles Taylor would caution against making any hasty assumptions about what is "commonsensical" when it comes to truth. An entire "picture" of knowledge that is relatively "new" (i.e., modern) has seeped down into our folk consciousness so that a representationalist account of knowing is *now* "commonsensical." But that doesn't mean it is *natural*.

Plantinga seems to appreciate something like this. So he summarizes the postmodern defeater in this way: "There is one common postmodern sort of view of truth according to which what is true depends on what we human beings say or think"; and that, he adds, "*does* seem incompatible with Christian belief" because that claim would mean "whether it is true that there is such a person as God depends upon us and what we do or think."[32] Plantinga latches on to Rorty's provocative claim that "truth is what our peers will let us get away with saying."[33] In effect this would mean that "God depends on us for his existence"—or at least depends on our peers[34]—and "from a Christian perspective, that is wholly absurd. This way of thinking about truth, therefore, is incompatible . . . with Christian belief."[35]

Ultimately, I want us to feel the force of Plantinga's concern, but hold off before drawing his conclusion just yet. I wholly agree with him that any understanding of truth that would make God's existence dependent upon us would be incompatible with orthodox

---

32. Ibid., 424.

33. Ibid., 429, citing Richard Rorty, *Philosophy and the Mirror of Nature*, 176 (slightly amended). (We will deal with this claim in context in chap. 3 below.) Plantinga glosses this as follows: "Presumably Rorty's claim is that the truth of a belief or proposition depends in some important way on social reality of one sort or another; truth is in some way a function of society and what it does or would do. What is true 'for us,' then, will depend somehow on our own society" (*Warranted Christian Belief*, 431). But those qualifications (*in some important way; in some way; somehow*) are crucial. It is not at all clear, depending on how these qualifiers are understood, that *this* sort of claim is necessarily incompatible with Christian faith. Indeed, one could suggest that Plantinga's own account of warrant already absorbs something like these sorts of considerations. (Plantinga notes that his account of "warrant," as articulated in *Warrant and Proper Function*, makes warrant "*relative to* circumstances" [ibid., 428, emphasis added].)

34. Plantinga, *Warranted Christian Belief*, 429. In his APA address, Plantinga comments on Rorty's claim: "The idea is not, I take it, that our peers are both so splendidly informed and so fastidious that as a matter of fact they'll let us get away with saying something if and only if that thing is true" ("How to be an Anti-Realist," 50). It is true (ironically) that Rorty does *not* mean that our peers have "correspondent" knowledge of "the way things are," which then functions as a realism by proxy. However, as we will see in a more careful exposition of Rorty's argument, our peers will *not* just let us get away with anything, and that's because we inhabit a world that constrains us in some way. It's just that as soon as realists like Plantinga or Smith hear "constraint" language, they think the *only* account must be "correspondence." We'll return to these matters in chap. 4.

35. Plantinga, *Warranted Christian Belief*, 425.

Christian belief. But I'd like us to slow down the game film here and reconsider the moves that got us to his hasty conclusion. We need to be a little more careful with a few of them. First, we will want to confirm that the pragmatist tradition of Wittgenstein, Rorty, and Brandom really does argue that "what is true depends on what we human beings say or think" (as I think it does). Then, second, we need to carefully consider *why* these pragmatists make such claims, and whether those claims aren't in fact rooted in close attention to the conditions of our finitude and creaturehood. When we do so, I think we'll find that pragmatism is a robust philosophy of contingency that is wholly compatible with the Christian doctrine of creation—and even something of a prophetic reminder of the importance of the Creator/creature distinction. Third, we'll want to confirm whether they draw the sort of metaphysical conclusions from this that Plantinga attributes to them. For example, do they really mean to claim that the human, social conditions of knowing and truth claims are metaphysically creative? Or that unless humans *say* something "is true" that things don't *exist*?

Then, and only then, can we finally re-ask Plantinga's question: Is such a (pragmatist) view of truth inconsistent with Christian belief? But we'll also flip the script and ask, Is the "realist" picture proffered by Smith and Plantinga the best—or even the *only*—epistemological option for Christians? Or could there in fact be good *theological* reasons to raise questions about realism and the epistemology it assumes? Could there be reasons and resources, internal to Christian confession, that should prompt us to think differently about truth and knowledge?

Picturing Contingency and Solidarity: *Wendy and Lucy*

Those Christians who foment alarm about the threat of relativism often invoke "absolute truth" as both a casualty and antidote. What's threatened by relativism is "absolute" truth, and yet the only thing that can deliver us from relativism is "absolute" truth. The frequent and sloppy use of the qualifier "absolute" leads to a common confusion of "relativism" with sheer arbitrariness. So when someone encounters the claim that truth "is relative," this is what they *hear*: truth is *arbitrary*—anything goes. In response, Christians then invoke "absolute" truth as an insulator and buffer against such arbitrariness—without ever really explaining what the adjective "absolute" does when appended to "truth." What exactly does the qualifier "absolute" add to the word "truth"? And if something's being absolute means that it is absolved of relation (the technical sense of the word), then what could that mean for contingent, social *creatures* like us?

This Christian reaction to relativism, with its therapeutic deployment of "absolute" truth, is a symptom of a deeper theological problem: an inability to honor the contingency and dependence of our creaturehood.[36] There might even be something rather gnostic (and heretical) in this failure to own up to contingency; indeed, one could argue that the claim to such "absoluteness" is at the heart of the first sin in the garden.[37] Conversely, appreciating our created finitude as the condition under which we know (and were *made* to know) should compel us to appreciate the contingency of our knowledge without sliding into arbitrariness. Saying "It depends" is *not* the equivalent of saying "It's not true" or "I don't know." Owning up to our finitude is *not* tantamount to giving up on truth, revelation, or scriptural authority. It is simply to recognize the conditions of our knowledge that are coincident with our status as finite, created, social beings. And those conditions are pronounced "very good" by the Creator (Gen. 1:31). One reason Christians should take seriously the pragmatist tradition from Wittgenstein through Rorty up to Brandom is that it can be received as a rigorous philosophical account of finitude and contingency, attentive to the material, social conditions of human, creaturely knowing.

Is Christianity synonymous with "objectivity"? Can finite humans hold "absolute" truths? What if the gospel is "relatively" true? Isn't the truth of Christian faith *relative to* Jesus Christ? And isn't our understanding of that story *dependent upon* the faith narrated in Scripture and handed down by tradition? Recall, for example, Christian Smith's outline of "strong" social constructionism, as I summarized it earlier.

---

36. In this respect, *Who's Afraid of Relativism?* can be read as an extension of arguments I made about finitude and creaturehood in my earlier book *The Fall of Interpretation: Philosophical Foundations for a Creational Hermeneutic*, 2nd ed. (Grand Rapids: Baker Academic, 2012).

37. Nicholas J. Ansell, "The Call of Wisdom/The Voice of the Serpent: A Canonical Approach to the Tree of Knowledge," *Christian Scholar's Review* 31, no. 1 (2001): 31–57.

- It assumes that humans *constitute* our "reality,"
- that this act of "making" our world is inevitably *social* and thus depends on a community or society or "people,"
- that our knowledge of reality is therefore *relative to* the categories and concepts that our community gives us,
- and that this means we can never "know" whether our beliefs *correspond* to reality because there would be no way to step outside a community to check whether our categories "match" an *external* reality.

What if we took that as a description of how we are illumined by the Holy Spirit, as part of the body of Christ, given the right categories and concepts from God's self-revelation in Christ and the Scriptures, in such a way that we are enabled to finally see the truth about creation that is otherwise suppressed by unrighteousness (Rom. 1:18–23)? Isn't it the case that Jesus's promise that the Spirit will lead us into all truth (John 16:13) is commenced at Pentecost, which is simultaneously the sending of the Spirit and the constitution of the church as the body of Christ, the "society" of the Spirit? True knowledge *depends* on God's revelation, and receiving that revelation *depends* on the regenerating and illuminating power of the Spirit as the conditions for knowing, which requires being enfolded into that "people" who gather in worship, to hear the Word, illumined by the Spirit. Grasping the truth about God, the world, and ourselves is dependent upon being part of the "us" illumined by the Spirit, heirs to the gift of the Scriptures, and part of the community of interpretive practice that is the church (1 Cor. 2:6–16).[38] So, in a sense, the answer to the question "Is Christianity true?" is the scandalous reply: "It depends." It depends on the One in whom all things hold together (John 1:1–4; Col. 1:15–20).

North American Christianity is especially allergic to the relativism and contingency highlighted by pragmatism precisely because we have become a people who are bent on security, comfort, and autonomy. We are uncomfortable with the scandalous dependence of radical discipleship. We are functional deists and practical atheists

38. As succinctly summarized by Stanley Hauerwas and Sam Wells, "Through worship God trains his people to take the right things for granted." "The Gift of the Church and the Gifts God Gives It," in *The Blackwell Companion to Christian Ethics*, ed. Stanley Hauerwas and Samuel Wells (Oxford: Blackwell, 2006), 25.

who have drunk the Kool-Aid of American ideals of independence. That's not a *cause* for our epistemological assumptions, but it can partially explain how they've become "common sense." In that respect, I think an engagement with pragmatism can be an exercise in self-examination, prompting us to remember and retrieve core convictions of Christian orthodoxy that our regnant epistemologies have led us to forget. We might think about bringing Rorty to church because he has something to teach us.

If the Christian doctrine of creation and creaturehood includes a robust account of contingency and dependence, and if pragmatism is a philosophical account of that contingency and dependence, then I might suggest that Kelly Reichardt's film *Wendy and Lucy* is a powerful cinematic illustration of the same themes.

The entire narrative is carried on the back of Wendy, played marvelously by Michelle Williams. We first meet Wendy and her faithful dog, Lucy, indirectly: the camera is watching her through the trees. Seeing her obliquely through the forest filmically connotes a sense of her vulnerability. Is someone stalking her? Are *we*? Is this some God's-eye-view we have of her? Or are we along for the ride?

So we find her wandering alone with Lucy, off the beaten path—the soundtrack a melancholy humming somewhere between contentment and sadness. We can already sense both strength and fragility here. She has had the courage to set out on her own, to leave behind a life in Indiana and strike out by herself for new opportunities in Alaska. When we meet her en route, in the Pacific Northwest, her "independence" is not very secure. To the contrary, her situation is tenuous. Apart from Lucy, she is alone, driving a beat-up old Honda Civic that seems on the brink of giving up the ghost. The fragility of her situation is highlighted by constant glimpses of her makeshift ledger: a small spiral notebook that lays out her plans, calculating the cost of gas against her finite (very meager) resources. Any expense out of left field would ruin everything. This is what the opposite of "financial security" looks like.

Just a couple of minutes into the movie this vulnerability and fragility is crystallized: in a split second, Lucy is gone. Searching for her, Wendy is now the one who is peering through the trees upon a group of vagabonds gathered around a fire, threatening and unpredictable. But they have Lucy. With a gulp, she approaches, and before long we realize her fears are unfounded. The vagabonds are well acquainted with grief, and dependence. Recognizing Wendy's need, they offer help, because it turns out they share something in common: they're all just passing through. This is a constant refrain from Wendy, a repeated phrase in the sparse dialogue of the film: "I'm just kind of passin' through." And as this phrase keeps being repeated, the constant sounds and images of trains begin to make sense: the squeal and rumble and whistle of the trains are the visualization of "passin' through." After all, who isn't?

In the graciousness of the vagabonds, who are also just "passin' through," we are confronted with the fact that our sense of threat is something *we* projected onto them because of their failure to conform to the ideals of responsible autonomy and security. Because they don't conform to our image of "stability" and normality, we imagine them threatening. If Wendy peered through the trees and saw Lucy with a nice suburban family laughing beside their backyard pool, we would have never given it a second thought. But the fact is, these vagabonds are not the pretty people we're used to. Indeed, Reichardt's film turns the gaze of the camera on a side of North American life we don't usually see in pictures: those vulnerable places on the other side of the tracks, without the glitz and pristine gleam of the new and suburban and respectable. This is a world without financial security and the autonomy of the middle class; instead, we see those who live on the edge, surviving, dependent on the help of others but also on good fortune, because they are all only one curveball away from ruin.[39]

And yet those who are dependent and vulnerable also don't seem to harbor the illusion of being otherwise—the illusions of security and independence that are part and parcel of our bourgeois "normality." As dependent, they recognize the dependence of others and are willing to give out of their own dependence. The motley crew at the bottle return depot is welcoming and ready to help Wendy. Even the CVS security guard is far from secure; he too is barely scraping by on a part-time, minimum-wage job. And yet he will press seven dollars into Wendy's hand as a gift, and you know it's the equivalent of the widow's mite.

39. The "soundtrack" of the film accords with the thinness of resources of the characters: no pop songs or indie ballads, just the screech and whistle of trains and the occasional humming.

Ruin becomes Wendy's story. She was held above it by only the slenderest of threads, and soon enough circumstances snap that thread: she sleeps in her car, but upon waking, her car won't start, which means a costly repair. That means she doesn't have enough money to eat—or feed Lucy, who is as dependent on Wendy as Wendy is on the cosmos. So in a moment of weakness, she steals some food. Caught for shoplifting,[40] she is hauled away to jail, which means that Lucy is abandoned for hours. And upon return, Lucy is gone. Without a car to find her, Wendy trudges miles and miles on foot. When her car is towed into the lot for repair, it means she has lost her shelter for sleeping, and so now she is even more exposed—sleeping outside, which leads to a harrowing scene of danger and threat, a terrifying scene of vulnerability. Still frantically searching for Lucy, she begins leaving articles of her clothing where Lucy might find them. So now Wendy is shedding the last remaining possessions she has; she is down to the shirt on her back and just a few dollars in her pocket.

But finally, some good news: Lucy is found. She had been welcomed by an adoptive family, a kind of canine foster care. Offloading the unrepairable car, settling her bill with the mechanic, and spending her last bit of money on a cab to Lucy, Wendy finds her faithful friend in a simple but idyllic home: a kindly gentleman to care and provide for her, a yard with room for Lucy to romp. And Wendy makes the hardest decision: to let Lucy go. Recognizing her own dependence, Wendy realizes the reality of Lucy's dependence on her and makes the heartbreaking decision to entrust her to this new caretaker—someone on whom the dog can depend.

As we see her hop into a boxcar with just a knapsack left to her name, we realize Lucy's relation to Wendy is like Wendy's relation to the cosmos: might someone adopt *her*, welcome *her*, provide for *her*?

---

40. The sixteen-year-old kid who catches Wendy and lobbies for her arrest is later picked up by his mom in the safety and security of the family's Volvo wagon. The automobiles are allegories in this movie. This same teenager voices the viewpoint of staid middle-class security when, pronouncing judgment on Lucy, he states: "If a person can't afford dog food, she shouldn't have a dog." Who can argue with that kind of economic logic?

A Christian Philosophy of Contingency

The church is most faithful, Stanley Hauerwas argues, when we "are content to live 'out of control.' For to be out of control means Christians can risk trusting in gifts, so they have no reason to deny the contingent character of our existence."[41] In other words, to know God is God (and we are *not*) is to own up to the tenuous fragility of our existence. This is to recognize that *everything* depends—not just our life and breath, but also truth and knowledge, even our epistemology and metaphysics. But all too often we construct accounts of knowledge and truth that effectively deny our dependence, that efface our vulnerability and try to "secure" us from the relativity of being a (rational, knowing) creature.

This is why I think pragmatism could actually be a gift to the church and its philosophers. Pragmatism is a philosophy of contingency; but it is also (*because* of that) a philosophy of community— a philosophical account of knowledge and truth that recognizes the essential link between dependence and community, contingency and solidarity. And *that* intuition, I would argue, is an essentially *creational* insight: it amounts to nothing less than a philosophical appreciation for the lineaments of creaturehood.

Embracing contingency does not entail embracing "liberalism": in fact, to the contrary, it is when we deny our contingency that we are thereby licensed to deny our dependence and hence assume the position where *we* are arbitrators of truth. We then spurn our dependence on tradition and assume a stance of "objective" knowledge whereby we can dismiss aspects of Scripture and Christian orthodoxy as benighted and unenlightened. In short, it is the denial of dependence that undergirds a progressive agenda. The picture of knowledge bequeathed to us by the Enlightenment is a forthright denial of our dependence, and it yields a God-like picture of human reason. It is "objectivity" that is "liberal."

Granted, there are two different ways of emphasizing contingency. As Hauerwas elsewhere notes, liberals often *do* emphasize that "everything is contingent." But he also notes an odd tension

41. Stanley Hauerwas, "Reforming Christian Social Ethics: Ten Theses," in *The Hauerwas Reader*, ed. John Berkman and Michael Cartwright (Durham, NC: Duke University Press, 2001), 113.

at that point: such a claim is less liberal and more nihilist. In contrast, the Christian claim about contingency is not that *everything* is contingent but rather that everything *created* is contingent.[42] Everything created depends upon the Triune Creator who, alone, is necessary. And that makes all the difference, Hauerwas points out, because it means that the Christian understanding of contingency is itself dependent. "The liberal nihilists are, of course, right that our lives are contingent," he says, "but their account of contingency is unintelligible. Contingent to what? If everything is contingent, then to say we are contingent is simply not interesting. In contrast, Christians know their contingency is a correlative to their status as creatures. To be contingent is to recognize that our lives are intelligible only to the extent that we discover we are characters in a narrative we did not create."[43] And that very discovery, I would add, depends upon our being "in Christ."

This book is an essay exploring the implications of this basic intuition about creaturely contingency and dependence for our accounts of knowledge and truth. At the same time, it is an extended philosophical conversation with pragmatism because I see pragmatism as a scrupulous philosophical account of the contingency, dependence, and sociality that characterizes human creaturehood. As such, the pragmatism of Wittgenstein, Rorty, and Brandom provides important resources to develop not a hip, relevant, contemporary "postmodern" account of truth "for our times" but rather an account of knowledge and truth that remembers and re-appreciates the implications of a biblical doctrine of creation. In other words, I'm not extolling pragmatism as a way for the church to "update" our account of knowledge and "get with the times" so that we can be "relevant" in a postmodern age. To the contrary, I'm arguing that a Christian philosophical engagement with pragmatism can be an occasion to remember core themes of Christian orthodoxy that we have effectively forgotten in modernity.

The structure of the book is relatively simple. On the one hand it is simply chronological, devoting a chapter to each key figure beginning with Wittgenstein, then Rorty, and finally Brandom. But

---

42. A claim carefully explicated by Thomas Aquinas in his little metaphysical work *De ente et essentia*.

43. Stanley Hauerwas, "Preaching as Though We Had Enemies," *First Things*, May 1995, 9.

this order is also a kind of conceptual snowball. It is Wittgenstein who crystallizes the core pragmatist insight that "meaning is use." Richard Rorty builds upon this, and emphasizes the *social* aspects of knowledge and truth that follow from Wittgenstein's insight. Then Robert Brandom teases out how we should think of reason and logic in light of Wittgenstein and Rorty.

Throughout these expositions I will also consider how and where the insights of pragmatism intersect with a Christian understanding of creaturehood and contingency, including an extensive comparison of Augustine and Wittgenstein at the conclusion of chapter 2. Finally, in chapter 5, we will explore the implications of a "Christian pragmatism" for Christian theology and ministry. This is embodied in George Lindbeck's notion of "postliberalism," including his timely proposals regarding the shape of evangelism, mission, and apologetics.

2

Community as Context

Wittgenstein on "Meaning as Use"

Not too many people sign up to be "relativists." It's not the sort of thing you announce on T-shirts or broadcast with a tattoo. It's usually a description "we" foist on others, a label to be applied to those with whom we disagree.

The story we tell about "relativism" is rooted in a story we usually don't articulate but still assume: a specific "picture" of *how* we know. And as Christian Smith rightly discerned, that account of knowing (epistemology) is bound up with a particular "picture" of what language is and how it works. So if we are going to grapple with the philosophical issues at stake in the vicinity of relativism, we need to spend most of our time dealing with the philosophy of language and philosophical issues related to meaning. These are issues at the heart of pragmatism in the wake of Wittgenstein's *Philosophical Investigations*.

If pragmatism can be described as a kind of relativism, this isn't because pragmatists are eager to sign up for wishy-washy sloppiness and soppy, sophomoric versions of "well-that-might-be-true-for-you" reasoning. The "relativism" that is articulated by the pragmatist tradition from Wittgenstein, through Rorty, up to Brandom is predicated on a distinctly philosophical critique of the epistemological picture that underwrites *realism*—specifically, the *representationalist* account of language and meaning. So if I am asking us to consider the (relative) virtues of pragmatism—and entertain the possibility of a "Christian pragmatism," maybe even a "Christian relativism"—it's not because I'm eager to sign up for the wishy-washy-ness of a "do-as-you-please" relativism, but rather because I think pragmatism is a better philosophical account of the creaturely conditions of knowing. Pragmatism is a philosophy that is attentive to our dependence in ways that realism and representationalism are not. This is why I think the default assumption that Christians should be "realists" deserves to be called into question, because you only get "realism" where you begin from "representationalism." And representationalism is a bad philosophical starting point for a host of reasons we'll explore—not least, I'll argue, because it seems to be an epistemology that is bent on overcoming creaturehood.[1]

This is what brings us to Ludwig Wittgenstein, whose work on logic, language, and meaning looms over philosophy in the twentieth century—and is the basis for the subsequent critique of realist representationalism. While Wittgenstein's life engenders fascination, I am going to focus on an exposition of his seminal work, the *Philosophical Investigations*.[2] This landmark "book"[3]—an almost aphoristic collection of insights and thought projects—is written as a critique of Wittgenstein's earlier work, the *Tractatus Logico-Philosophicus*, which in many ways embodies the realist representationalism that Wittgenstein rejects. In other words, in the *Investigations*, Wittgenstein is criticizing his younger representationalist self. Since it is just this representationalism that undergirds

1. At the very least we should recognize that representationalist epistemology is a contingent development in the history of philosophy and thus can't possibly be the necessary presupposition of any authentic "Christian" philosophy. If that were the case, then Augustine couldn't have been a Christian philosopher!

2. Wittgenstein has proved a source of cultural fascination beyond the narrow confines of professional philosophy. See, for example, Alexander Waugh's remarkable portrait of the family in *The House of Wittgenstein: A Family at War* (New York: Doubleday, 2009). Consider also David Markson's novel *Wittgenstein's Mistress* (Champaign, IL: Dalkey Archive Press, 1988). A 2012 edition includes David Foster Wallace's essay "The Empty Plenum: David Markson's *Wittgenstein's Mistress*" as an afterword (243–75).

3. As Wittgenstein himself noted in the preface, "This book is really only an album." See Ludwig Wittgenstein, *Philosophical Investigations*, 3rd ed., trans. G. E. M. Anscombe (New York: Macmillan, 1953), v; henceforth abbreviated as *PI*.

the "realism" that so staunchly rejects relativism, we will trace the thread of Wittgenstein's argument in order to consider just why we might want to give up being "realists."

"Meaning as Use": Breaking the Spell of Representation

Wittgenstein opens the *Philosophical Investigations* by targeting a particular "picture" of language. This picture or model of language will seem "commonsensical" to us, but Wittgenstein will try to show that, in fact, this is a "picture" of language that we have learned. And he will try to help us *un*learn it.

This "particular picture of the essence of human language" can be described as a "naming" theory of language: "individual words in language name objects," and sentences are just collections of such names (*PI*, §1).[4] Assuming this picture of language, we then generate a corresponding account of meaning: "Every word has a meaning. This meaning is correlated with the word. It is the object for which the word stands" (*PI*, §1). Meaning, in other words, is the correlation between a word and a thing. Meaning is *reference*: a word refers to a thing and the "hook" between the two is "meaning." Words are pointers, and words *mean* just to the extent that they correctly point to the *things* that concern us. That's what we mean by "meaning." We might call this a "referentialist" theory of language.

This seems so intuitive as to be obvious. But Wittgenstein immediately calls into question the adequacy of this picture of meaning. He does so by means of a little vignette that is meant to highlight a "use of language" that can't be explained by means of the "picture" theory.

> I send someone shopping. I give him a slip marked "five red apples."
> He takes the slip to the shopkeeper, who opens the drawer marked
> "apples"; then he looks up the word "red" in a table and finds

4. Wittgenstein suggests this is a very "noun-ish" picture of language: "If you describe the learning of language in this way you are, I believe, thinking primarily of nouns like 'table,' 'chair,' 'bread,' and of peoples' names, and only secondarily of the names of certain actions and properties; and of the remaining kinds of words as something that will take care of itself" (*PI*, §1). In other words, it's a little hard to know what *thing* the word "or" corresponds to.

a colour sample opposite it; then he says the series of cardinal numbers—I assume that he knows them by heart—up to the word "five" and for each number he takes an apple of the same colour as the sample out of the drawer. It is in this and similar ways that one operates with words. (*PI*, §1)

This is an odd shopkeeper, no? Sounds more like a robot with only minimal artificial intelligence. In any case, with this kind of slow-motion view of human interaction, Wittgenstein is trying to test out the adequacy of the "picture" theory of language and the referentialist account of meaning. So far so good: the word "apples" refers to the crisp fruits in that drawer over there; the word "red" refers to the sheen of those apples that sort of look like firetrucks; and the word "five" refers to a number. So the shopkeeper seems to be a good example of how words mean: by reference.

But at this point Wittgenstein makes a common move in the *Philosophical Investigations* and sort of becomes his own inter-locutor, playing devil's advocate with himself.

"But how does he know where and how he is to look up the word 'red' and what he is to *do* with the word 'five'?" Well, I assume that he *acts* as I have described. Explanations comes to an end somewhere. But what is the meaning of the word "five"?—No such thing was in question here, only how the word "five" is used. (*PI*, §1)

There's a little chink in the armor of the representationalist account here: it is the challenge of number. Is "five" a *thing*? Just what "thing" is referred to by the word "five?" If you picture the Arabic numeral "5," that's not quite right, since that is just another sign for the concept "five." So Wittgenstein now has us wondering: Does language always work by *referring*? Or are there other *uses* of language that can't be accounted for by the "naming" picture of language? Indeed, you can already hear Wittgenstein express-ing his doubts when he asks: How did the shopkeeper know what to *do* with the note? How did he know the note meant "*give me five red apples*"? Wittgenstein is interested in how the shopkeeper *acts*—what he *does* with the note. What the note *means* seems to be more than what the words might *point* to.

Wittgenstein presses this point by means of a second scenario or illustration. Imagine, he says, a language meant to serve as a means of communication between builder A and his assistant B.

Let's call them Albert and Barney for our discussion here. Albert is building with a collection of different stones: blocks, pillars, slabs, and beams. Barney's job is to bring the appropriate stones to Albert when he needs them. "For this purpose," Wittgenstein describes, "they use a language consisting of the words 'block,' 'pillar,' 'slab,' 'beam.'" So you can picture the scene: Albert is up on the scaffold barking out curt orders: "Slab!" he shouts. Then Barney "brings the stone which he has learnt to bring at such-and-such a call" (*PI*, §2).

This scene is a compact rendition of the referentialist picture of language: there are words ("pillar," "block," "slab") and there are things (pillars, blocks, and slabs) and Barney knows the meaning of "Slab!" when he connects the right word to the right thing. Meaning *is* just reference on this picture, and understanding is a kind of connect-the-dots affair—like one of those "matching" questions on middle school history tests.

But is that really an adequate account of meaning in this scenario? Does Barney really "understand" Albert if he rightly correlates the word "slab" with the rectangular piece of stone lying there in the pile? What if every time Albert shouts "Slab!" Barney looks at the rectangular piece of stone, and every time Albert shouts "Pillar!" Barney dutifully looks at the cylindrical piece of stone? Would this not be sufficient to indicate that Barney "understands" Albert? After all, he has clearly matched the word with the thing; he knows which words *refer* to which things. So he must get the *meaning* of Albert's words, right?

Well, ask Albert! Having worked as a bricklayer's assistant, I can tell you that if I simply correlated the word to the thing when the brickie was shouting commands, I would have been not-so-politely asked to not bother coming back (there may have been some cussing involved). Albert would not think the mere correlation of reference would count as "understanding" what he said. No, when he shouts "Slab!" he expects Barney to *bring* him a slab. This is why it's crucial to note an important but understated feature of Wittgenstein's scenario: he tells us that they come up with this language *for a purpose*. They are engaged in the common labor of building something. There is an *end* to which they are working in collaboration. They are trying to get something *done*. The language is instrumental to an end; they use it in order to accomplish something. This is why Barney only rightly understands when he *acts* in response. What "Slab!" means is relative to—and dependent upon—the context in which it is employed. This is the turning point in Wittgenstein's alternative account of language and meaning. And it's why we're all relativists.

So the question is, How does Barney learn this language? Does "understanding" the language just amount to learning *reference*, the correlation between words and things? If that were the case, then we would learn a language—and hence learn "meaning"— entirely by *pointing*. Or, as Wittgenstein puts it, all language teaching would boil down to "ostensive" teaching—that is, teaching by *pointing*. The ostensive teaching of words is what we do with tiny toddlers: we hold up a ball and say, "Ball." (For some reason, we usually say it in slow motion with just a hint of doubt: "Baaaallll?") We point to the cat and say, "Cat." We point to Mommy and say, "Mommy." Such teaching establishes "an association between the word and the thing" (*PI*, §6). If meaning is reference and thus teaching meaning is teaching association, then the toddler is beginning to understand if she pictures a ball when someone says "ball." And she will exhibit that understanding when she picks up the round object in front of her and says, to the delight of everyone, "Ball?"

Wittgenstein recognizes that this happens; he's just not convinced that this actually counts as understanding. Which is why he asks: "But now, if this does happen—is it the *purpose* of the word?" Or, to return to Albert and Barney: "If the ostensive teaching has this effect—am I to say it effects an understanding of the word? Don't you *understand* the call 'Slab!' if you *act* upon it in such-and-such a way?" (*PI*, §6, emphasis added). In which case, the meaning of "Slab!" is not just word association, a matter of getting the right picture in your head when you hear the word. This would certainly be Albert's position on the matter.

Now you might protest: of course the call "Slab!" is only fully understood if Barney actually brings Albert the slab. But even then, he first has to correlate the word to the right block of stone. So in fact reference or correlation is the *basis* for the fuller understanding that involves Barney acting in the right way. While understanding might sometimes involve more than reference, it seems to always involve *at least* reference as its basis. So even "contextual" understanding is at root referentialist.

Wittgenstein's not buying it, for this reason: You can only learn by pointing if you've already learned a host of things that were never pointed at. In other words, training in reference is actually built on a complex web of training and learning that is not ostensive. And in fact all of this non-ostensive training has to be in place for you to be able to learn by pointing. You can only learn meaning as reference if you have *already* learned all kinds of other modes of meaning that no one has ever pointed at or pointed out. Ostensive training is always already embedded in a broader, prior training that is bound up with a community of practice with ends and goals and purposes. This kind of training is caught more than taught, if you know what I mean: we absorb such understanding *in practice*, without any ostensive definition.

For example, think of the woman teaching her daughter that the spherical shape in front of her is a ball. She points to the object and says to her daughter, "Ball." She does so over and over again, establishing the association. And eventually her daughter will make the connection—will understand the reference—and say "ball" when she wants to play with the spherical object (and/or please her mother). But how did the baby know that this act of pointing-and-saying was meant to encourage such association?[5] Did the mother point to her pointing and teach the child the principle of association?[6]

Return now to Wittgenstein's earlier example (§1): When the shopkeeper received the note with "five red apples," he certainly associated the words with things and concepts. But he didn't just picture these things in his head, nod politely, and return the note. He went to the drawer and retrieved five red apples. But how did he know—and how did he *learn*—that the note *meant* he should *do* that? Here Wittgenstein wants us to appreciate two features of our language use, and hence the dynamics of meaning.

First, language is *used* for something. It is employed for some end, spoken within a community of practice that has some *telos*, that is trying to get something done (even if the "doing" in some instances might be theoretical reflection). Language use is always caught up in teleological communities of practice, which means that even reference and ostensive teaching are always already embedded in wider contexts of action and practice. Second, in some sense language and meaning are *bigger* than words. Language and

---

5. Try pointing to something with your cat, and see if it makes the same association.
6. Or as Wittgenstein asks, "Are 'there' and 'this' also taught ostensively?" (§9).

meaning are bound up with a context of practice that is more than the repertoire of our words, and that penumbra of practices and action is essential to constituting the meaning of our words.[7] Words mean more than we say precisely because meaning is wider than words. Or as Wittgenstein puts it later, "To imagine a language means to imagine a form of life" (§19).

To get at this wider sense of language and meaning, Wittgenstein introduces the notion of "language-games" to encompass "the whole, consisting of language and the actions into which it is woven" (§7). A language-game is the practical context in which our words and speech make sense—which is why understanding is bound up with, and relative to, the practical *telos* of the language-game, the *end* to which a community of practice is oriented. If Barney is going to understand Albert, for example, it's not enough for him to master a lexicon by ostensive definition; he needs to be trained how to play the stonemason language-game. That involves absorbing an understanding of what we're *doing*. Barney needs to be inculcated into this community of practice, needs to learn to play this game, which will require that he learn all kinds of *un*spoken aspects of the game that are never taught ostensively but rather "caught" as we participate in a community of practice.

To be a good understand-er, then, is not just to be a good word-association-ist.[8] To understand, you actually need to be a competent *practitioner*; you need to know how to play the (language-) game; you need to have been inducted into the community of practice. You

---

7. Thus in the "five red apples" example, Wittgenstein says we need to count the color samples as "part of the language" (§16).

8. In this context Wittgenstein has a long consideration of just what counts as a "word" anyway. For example, he says (§§19–20), imagine a foreigner who happens upon a worksite where the stonemason regularly shouts, "Bring me a slab!" As a non-competent practitioner of the language, this foreigner is nonetheless a close observer, and over time he begins to make the association between "Bring me a slab!" and the laborer carrying a rectangular piece of stone to the mason. So he builds up a "correct" sense of reference. But he actually thinks "Bring me a slab!" is one word: "Bringmeaslab." So he thinks "bringmeaslab" *is* "the" word that correlates with retrieving the rectangular stone thing. Does that mean he does *not* understand? Only if we buy into the noun-ish, referentialist picture of language. But if by chance the foreigner is hired as a laborer, in fact we'll see that he can function in this community of practice because he knows what to *do*. The association of a discrete word is less relevant than understanding what he is supposed to do with the words in this game. The different "interior" conceptions of what the mason is saying and what the foreigner hears do not seem to be relevant.

need to know *why* we're saying what we're saying, and you need to have a sense of what we're about, what we're after because meaning—even ostensive or referentialist meaning—is ultimately dependent upon the conventions of a community of practice. "Sense," or meaning, then, is bound up with *use*, and use is relative to the conventions of a community of practitioners (or "players" of a language-game). Wittgenstein's introduction of the notion of a "language-game" is "meant to bring into prominence the fact that the *speaking* of language is part of an activity, or of a form of life" (§23). Hence ultimately, in almost all cases, "the meaning of a word is its use in the language" (§43).

One of the upshots of Wittgenstein's account is to see language as something we use and deploy in a range of ways, for all sorts of different ends, and not just to point to things. In other words, language is not only—and not even fundamentally—indicative. Language isn't just for referring or pointing or claiming. Language isn't only or even fundamentally for making assertions or articulating propositional claims. We *do* many things with words beyond assertion and making indicative claims. This insight resonates with what we now know as "speech act" theory, which sees language as a mode of action that can be used to accomplish all sorts of things.[9]

In this context, Wittgenstein introduces an important metaphor of language as a city. While referentialist theories of meaning might recognize that there could be other uses of language, they will ardently insist that assertions (indicative claims) are at the heart of language: they are the "downtown" of language.[10] All other uses, then, are "suburbs" of language (§18). But in Wittgenstein's account, language is more like an "ancient city: a maze of little streets and squares, of old and new houses, and of houses with additions from various periods; and this surrounded by a multitude of new boroughs with straight regular streets and uniform houses"—but no "downtown" that constitutes the heart or "foundation" of language use. Instead, use is as malleable and adaptive

9. See J. L. Austin, *How to Do Things with Words*, 2nd ed. (Cambridge, MA: Harvard University Press, 1975); and John Searle, *Speech Acts: An Essay in the Philosophy of Language* (Cambridge: Cambridge University Press, 1970). For an extensive engagement with speech act theory from a Christian perspective, see Nicholas Wolterstorff, *Divine Discourse: Philosophical Reflections on the Claim That God Speaks* (Cambridge: Cambridge University Press, 1995).

10. We will see this issue return in Brandom's critique of Wittgenstein.

as the multitude of activities that we undertake, morphing and
stretching, expanding and adding as we go.

To observe that "meaning is use" is to recognize that meaning
is always game-relative—which is to say that meaning is always
conventional. It depends; more specifically, meaning depends on
the conventions of a community of practice—what Wittgenstein
variously describes as a "language-game" or a "form of life."[11] The
locus of meaning is not the line that connects the dots of a word
to a thing; rather, the locus of meaning is an entire web of communal practice and conventions. What "Slab!" means is not simply
found in the correspondence of the word with a thing; neither is
the meaning resident in the mind of the utterer, since in shouting
"Slab!" Albert is already joining a game in progress. He is indebted
to a community and at the same time is able to marshal the gifts
of convention in order to get something done. So the claim that
"meaning is use" is, at root, a deeply *social* account of meaning.
If we can describe this as a "relativism"—since it makes meaning
relative to a form of life—we should not mistake it for a subjectivism. Meaning is not relative *to me*; it is relative to the conventions
of a community. Indeed, for Wittgenstein there is no "I" that is not
always already indebted to a community of practice. Solipsism is
simply an impossibility.

We could say that Albert is able to deploy the *name* "slab" because he has acquired competence—a know-*how*—with names in
the context of a community of practice. He knows how to make a
move in a language-game with the piece "slab." He has been inculcated into the language-game in such a way that he understands
the purpose or goal of the game, and now words are part of the
wider "language" that he employs to play that game. He names
things in order to *do* something. Knowing what to do with words
is dependent upon an unspoken and unarticulated know-*how*. So
too with Barney: he is only able to learn the "definition" of "slab"
because he has absorbed the halo of meanings and significance
that surround it in the very task of constructing the building. The
acquisition of know-*how* is a prerequisite for knowing-*what*—for

---

11. As we will see below, this does *not* mean that the community can just "mean"
anything it wants. To note that convention is a necessary condition of meaning is
not to claim that it is the *only* condition. This is why Wittgenstein's "relativism" is
not an arbitrary-ism. We will return to such matters in our engagement with Rorty.

naming. Thus Wittgenstein concludes: "One has already to know (or be able to do) something in order to be capable of asking a thing's name. But what does one have to know?" (*PI*, §30).

To get at this question, he introduces another example: someone teaching another the game of chess. Consider all of the ostensive (i.e., referential) training that goes on in this case. "This is the bishop; this is a pawn; this is the king," and so on. But once again, Wittgenstein notes that such ostensive/referentialist training will only be effective if there has already been some other induction into games—a certain know-how that the learner already brings to this discussion. "When one shows someone the king in chess and says: 'This is the king,' this does not tell him the use of this piece—unless he already knows the rules of the game up to this last point: the shape of the king" (*PI*, §31). In other words, there has to be a great deal of spade work done before the ostensive instruction "This is the king" is really going to teach the learner anything. Once again, referentialist meaning is dependent upon a know-how that is bound up with *use*. Unless I know what a king is *for*, the instruction that "This is the king" will be largely meaningless. Only if I already bring with me some sense of what games are will I be able to be instructed in what are legitimate moves in *this* game. "The words 'This is the king' (or 'This is called the "king"') are a definition only if the learner already 'knows what a game piece is'" (§31). Reference is always already dependent on other modes of meaning and know-how.

In fact, Wittgenstein entertains the possibility of "someone's having learnt the game without ever learning or formulating the rules" (§31). What he seems to mean here is that someone could have so absorbed the rules of the game that they could be a "master of the game" and yet lack the ability to *articulate* that know-how. Such a prodigy might not be able to play the referentialist/ostensive game of correlating names with pieces and yet still know *how* to move them. In that case I will have mastered the conventions and purposes of the community of practitioners, and thus understand what I am supposed to *do*. And if meaning is *use*, then this means I can understand the meaning without having to articulate it in terms of reference. Meaning *precedes* reference rather than being equated with it. This will have serious implications for "realism" precisely because it is rooted in the sort of referentialism that Wittgenstein deconstructs.

Contextualizing Reference

If analytic philosophy is defined by breaking down issues into their smallest components—reducing complexity to atomistic matters of definition in order to achieve clarity—then Wittgenstein is decidedly *not* an "analytic" philosopher. In fact, he refuses to reduce meaning to something simple or atomistic like naming or reference. Thus later philosophers in the Wittgensteinian line—like Wilfrid Sellars, Rorty, and Brandom—have described Wittgenstein's approach as a "holism": instead of reducing meaning to small basic units like individual words or signs, Wittgenstein presses us to see how we *use* language and thus recognize that we utter sentences, not discrete words.[12]

It's worth noting something about Wittgenstein's idiosyncratic method on this point. Since he is arguing that meaning is use, he is constantly trying to direct our attention to how we actually use language. This requires pushing back against a very bad habit that philosophers have: treating ordinary human beings as if they were all philosophers. In this case, Wittgenstein is trying to counter the habit of painting language users in the image of representationalists, because he is convinced that if we actually attend to linguistic practice we will find that representation plays only a marginal role. And thus he constantly grabs us by the shoulders, shakes us vigorously, and effectively says: "Take off your philosophical blinders and *look*! Stop looking at human practice through representational-colored glasses and just attend to how language is actually deployed in ordinary practice." His goal is to disabuse us of what he calls "philosophical superstition" (§49), by which he means the fabrication of theories that don't pay attention to practice, to "ordinary language."[13] So Wittgenstein is constantly pressing us to stop letting our theories blind us to what's right in front of us. As he bluntly puts it: "Don't think, but look!" (§66). "In order to see more clearly, here as in countless similar cases, we must focus on the details of what goes on; must look at them

12. Wilfrid Sellars, longtime professor of philosophy at the University of Pittsburgh, influenced both Rorty and Brandom. His most seminal work is *Empiricism and the Philosophy of Mind*, with an introduction by Richard Rorty and a study guide by Robert Brandom (Cambridge, MA: Harvard University Press, 1997).

13. E.g., in §§151–84, Wittgenstein tries to disabuse us of the philosophical superstition of "interior" mental life as necessary for making sense of meaning.

from close to" (§51). Wittgenstein is trying to help us look at our linguistic practice more closely.

And when we do, he believes, we will see that it is not *words* that are the "basic unit" of language, but rather sentences. In other words, "naming" comes second. Recall Wittgenstein's opening critique: we have unwittingly bought into a referentialist picture of language in which words are taken to be names of things. In that referentialist model, words/signs/names are the basic unit of language, and sentences are just collections of names. So we start with word-thing correlations and then put those together to make up sentences that are collections of word-thing associations. Let's call this an "atomistic" picture: words are like atoms and sentences are like molecules of meaning—collections of names.

But Wittgenstein has already shown that naming or reference is always already embedded in other modes of meaning ("use"). Naming is not basic, which means that word-things are not basic. So in contrast to this atomistic picture, Wittgenstein offers a *holistic* account where sentences precede words because it is *sentences* that constitute moves within a language-game. It is in the utterance of sentences that we communicate and get things done.

> For naming and describing do not stand on the same level: naming is a preparation for description. Naming is so far not a move in the language-game—any more than putting a piece in its place on the board is a move in chess. We may say: *nothing* has so far been done, when a thing has been named. It has not even *got* a name except in the language-game. This was what Frege meant too, when he said that a word had a meaning only as part of a sentence. (§49)

"Naming" (which Wittgenstein takes to be synonymous with reference) is not really even a move in a language-game because it doesn't really get anything done. It's more like putting a piece on the board. In fact, a word only functions *as* a name against the background of its use in a language-game.

Wittgenstein is not denying that naming/reference has a place; he is offering what we might call a "deflationary" account of reference. Whereas representationalist models see naming/association/reference as fundamental, Wittgenstein sees it as secondary and relatively insignificant. Most importantly, correspondence or reference is itself game-dependent. What counts as correspondence is a connection that is game-relative. Correspondence is conventional (§51).[14]

Now, once again, we need to resist the temptation here to launch into indignant tirades about how Wittgenstein's account will mean "anything goes," erasing any sense of "objective" reality and thus leading us into a la-la land of fantasy where we can just make everything up. To say that correspondence is a matter of convention is meant to emphasize two things. First, the connection between words and the world is *contingent*. Correspondences are not "natural" and could have been otherwise. That this red, rather spherical object in front of me is called an "apple" in English[15] is not something that is dictated or demanded by the material phenomenon on the table. It's not that the thing is there, "named" in the mind of God who is now waiting to see if we discover the *right* name. It's not like God has written down the name on a paper behind his back and is now waiting to see if we can guess what it is. ("Is it 'pumpkin'?" "No." "Um, is it, 'pupple'?" "No, but you're getting warmer!") To the contrary, even in the biblical narrative we see that humanity is tasked with naming the animals. Language, naming, and correspondence are features of a contingent cultural system unpacked and developed *by* humanity.[16]

Second, when we say that correspondence is a matter of convention, we are saying that it is a *social* phenomenon: it is a matter of agreement between language users. As a matter of convention, in order to get things done, a community of language users agrees that "apple" will be the name we give to these sorts of phenomena. If we were French, the agreement would be that *pomme* would serve this purpose. This is why Wittgenstein's account can be seen as "pragmatic": he ties meaning to *use* because he recognizes that language-games have a purpose. Our speaking, writing, hearing, and expressing are part and parcel of human being-in-the-world; we don't have language in order to merely comment on our world,

---

14. Below we will see that St. Augustine makes basically the same point.

15. This qualifier in itself should be enough to help us appreciate the contingency of such names. What if English had never emerged as a language? Then how could "apple" be the "right" name for this piece of the cosmos?

16. In "The Linguistic Turn as a Theological Turn," John Milbank argues that "Christian orthodoxy always encouraged the view that language was of human, rather than divine origin" (in *The Word Made Strange: Theology, Language, Culture* [Oxford: Blackwell, 1997], 84–113).

as if we were merely spectators. Language is bound up with our investment in cultural projects; it is part and parcel of our culture making. It is part of the web by which we make our way in the world. And our culture making is inherently communal and social. We are always already indebted to those around us and those who have gone before us, even if we take up their gifts in a way that is bent on denying our indebtedness. Any argument for solipsism, for example, can only be made by availing oneself of the linguistic system that is the product of a *community* of language users. Or on a political level: every revolutionary will be living off of the borrowed capital of the society against which he or she rails. Wittgenstein is pressing us to recognize that this communal situatedness is fundamental and precedes all of our meaning making as its condition of possibility. To be human is to be social, which is to be indebted, woven into a web of meaning making that is the product of social construction. This is why Wittgenstein later emphasizes that learning to speak and learning to know are aspects of *custom*, of a kind of training that is more like "socialization" into a people than the didactic ingestion of ideas (*PI*, §§198–219). This is also why we can recognize that correspondence is conventional without thereby casting ourselves into the abyss of sheer arbitrariness (as Christian Smith worries). To "deflate" correspondence and "situate" representation within the given web of social convention doesn't mean that there is no longer right or wrong. If you call this red fruit on the table a "pumpkin," you will be *wrong*—not because the sound "pumpkin" doesn't naturally or essentially correspond with the thing but because we, as a community of language users, have come to an agreement that we will use the sound "apple" to name this thing. And there is no naming or reference that isn't rooted in such convention. Community precedes correspondence. And this is a feature of finitude, a characteristic of creaturehood.

Family Resemblances and Blurred Concepts

I think one of the reasons why Wittgenstein makes us skittish is because a lot of philosophers are conceptual control freaks. The very task of analysis is bent on finding clean, crisp definitions and one-to-one concepts. So the very goal of "analytic" philosophy is to clarify our concepts: to discipline our fuzzy use of terms in order to achieve clarity and the (fabled) "rigor" that is the supposed outcome of such analysis.

Well, if this is your ideal of philosophy, Wittgenstein will give you fits. In fact, you can feel this in the *Investigations* itself, which lets us know that he is aware of the concern. For after his introduction of the notion of "language-games" and his account of meaning as use, Wittgenstein introduces the voice of an exasperated interlocutor who responds to Wittgenstein's argument with not a little frustration.

> You take the easy way out! You talk about all sorts of language-games, but have nowhere said what the essence of a language-game, and hence of language, is: what is common to all these activities and what makes them into language or parts of language. So you let yourself off the very part of the investigation that once gave you yourself most headache, the part about the *general form of propositions* and of language. (§65)

Wittgenstein is willing to concede the point: "This is true," he says. "Instead of producing something common to all that we call language, I am saying that these phenomena have no one thing in common which makes us use the same word for all,—but that they are *related* to one another in many different ways. And it is because of this relationship, or these relationships, that we call them all 'language'" (§65). Sensing his interlocutor's puzzlement, he promises to explain. The explanation, however, is not likely to satisfy, since the answer to this question will be Wittgenstein's defense of "fuzzy" concepts.

Wittgenstein asks us to stop expecting our practice to conform to some Platonic ideal and invites us instead to attend to what we actually *do*, how our language *works*. When we do so, we will find that we are more than able to manage without precise, crisp definitions. In fact, we *need* fuzzy concepts and depend on them in practice all the time. "Consider for example the proceedings that we call 'games.' I mean board-games, card-games, ball-games, Olympic games, and so on. What is common to them all?" (§66). And he immediately pushes back on our tendency to philosophical superstition—our tendency to impose Platonic expectations on our everyday experience. So he cautions, "Don't say: 'There *must* be something common, or they would not be called "games"'—but *look and see* whether there is something common to all" (§66).

When we *look* at our actual practice and *see* what we do, we will "not see something that is common to *all*, but similarities, relationship, and a whole series of them at that" (§66). Indeed, if you try to find that *one* thing that is common to solitaire, pole vault, musical chairs, and basketball, you're going to be stymied. Features that pole vault and basketball have in common won't hold for solitaire; and just when you think you've hit upon the one thing that is common to solitaire and musical chairs, you'll look in vain to find it in basketball, and so on. Instead of thinking that there must be *one* thing that defines the essence of a "game," we should look at our linguistic practice and recognize that we're able to deploy the word "game" in meaningful ways, across a range of instances, *without* defining such an essence. What is common here is not one essence but instead "a complicated network of similarities overlapping and criss-crossing: sometimes overall similarities, sometimes similarities of detail" (§66). Wittgenstein characterizes these complex but intuited similarities as "family resemblances": "for the various resemblances between members of a family: build, features, colour of eyes, gait, temperament, etc. etc. overlap and criss-cross in the same way" (§67). It is in this sense—and by means of this kind of similarity—that all of these diverse phenomena can be described as "games." And hence we can speak of language-games without having to define the "essence" of language.

Competent language users have no trouble managing this complex network and thus successfully deploying the word "game" in a whole host of contexts. *In practice*, we always know more than we can define. In practice, our words and concepts are not rigidly "bounded"; that is, the extension and employment of concepts "is *not* closed by a frontier" (§68). Now, you *can* do that if you want: you can rigidly stipulate a boundary for a concept. But your rigid stipulation will still be conventional and, in fact, rather arbitrary. The rigid stipulation of conceptual clarity will only work insofar as you get a community of linguistic practitioners to *agree* to that "definition" of the concept—in which case the definition is still conventional.

Rigidly defining and "clarifying" our concepts is a conventional exercise that doesn't mitigate the fact that, *in practice*, we manage our being-in-the-world with all sorts of conceptual fuzziness. We know what we mean—and can communicate with others—quite successfully without engaging in such conceptual boundary-drawing. "To repeat," Wittgenstein says, "we can draw a boundary—for a special purpose," say, logical analysis of propositions. But "does it take that to make the concept usable? Not at all! (Except for that special purpose.)" (§69). We all use the word "game" without being able to spit out an "essential" definition that would then give us permission to use it as a description of both solitaire and speed skating. In other words, we are able to *use* the concept without having the sort of one-to-one conceptual clarity that spells out the "essence" of a game. So maybe we should stop looking for such essences and recognize that even when we supposedly "find" them, we're only stipulating them according to some convention.

Does that mean there are *no* rules for the deployment of such concepts—that I can call just anything and everything a "game"? No, says Wittgenstein: Why is it always all or nothing for you?! To recognize that our concepts are not rigidly fixed or bounded is *not* to say that no rules apply or that "anything goes." It is not a question of *whether* our concepts are regulated but *how*. Wittgenstein tries to articulate this with an analogy from tennis: a concept "is not everywhere circumscribed by rules; but no more are there any rules for how high one throws the ball in tennis, or how hard; yet tennis is a game for all that and has rules too" (§68). Just because every little aspect of tennis is not governed by clear rules does not mean it is entirely *un*regulated. You have to land the ball within the lines; you can't step on the line when you serve; you can't catch it with your hands, and so on. There are parameters of play, but there are all sorts of aspects of the game that are unregulated: how high you can throw the ball on a serve, whether you use one hand or two on a backhand stroke, and so forth.

Wittgenstein's skeptical interlocutor who is bent on conceptual precision tends to take an all-or-nothing approach that simply doesn't square with how much fuzziness we accept in our practice (including analytic philosophers!). So the objector thinks that if there are no rigid conceptual boundaries, there is no concept; if we don't have a one-to-one definition, then we can't even know what we're talking about. "If the concept 'game' [and hence 'language-game'] is uncircumscribed like that," he objects, "you don't really know what you mean by a 'game'" (§70). But Wittgenstein would remind us of an earlier point: we are all masters of know-*how* that we can't articulate (§31). So he responds to his objector: "When I give the description: 'The ground was quite covered with plants'— do you want to say I don't know what I am talking about until I can give a definition of a plant?" (§70). The question is, "What does it mean to *know* what a game is? What does it mean, to know it and not be able to say it?" (§75, emphasis added).

The fact is, in our practice—which is meaningful and makes sense of our world—we *know* with concepts that have "blurred edges" (§71). Indeed, they only look "blurred" when we kick into the mode of analysis and are expecting a kind of clarity and precision that is artificial vis-à-vis our lived experience. The analyst is going to wonder whether a "blurred concept" is really a concept at all. But again, that is imposing an ideal upon our situated being-in-the-world that is not an issue in practice. In fact, Wittgenstein asks, "Is it even always an advantage to replace an indistinct picture by a sharp one? Isn't the indistinct one often exactly what we need?" (§71).[17] "Blurred concepts" can help us "get things done" in ways that sharp pictures may not.

Ultimately, Wittgenstein concludes, we're talking about two very different kinds of knowing. When you ask me to *define* a game— giving you a sharp picture, a concept that distills the essence—you are asking me to articulate my knowledge of games in a way that can be propositionalized. This is just the sort of articulation that will be necessary for logical analysis. It is propositional knowledge. And if, because I can't define a game *in this way*, you thereby conclude that I don't *know* what a game is—or worry that "we" can't *know* what a game is—this only indicates that you are working with a narrow notion of knowledge. You are effectively reducing all knowledge to propositional knowledge and assume (and thus demand) that any claim that is going to *count* must exhibit this kind of knowledge.

But Wittgenstein refuses to play along precisely because he recognizes multiple modes of knowing. He can recognize propositional knowledge—the sort that can be sharply defined—but he doesn't think this is the *only* mode of knowing, and he doesn't even think

17. Wittgenstein takes on Gottlob Frege on this point: "Frege compares a concept to an area and says that an area with vague boundaries cannot be called an area at all. This presumably means we cannot do anything with it.—But is it senseless to say: 'Stand roughly there'?" (§71).

it is either the most fundamental or the most important. Hear his question again: "What does it mean to know what a game is? What does it mean, to know it and not be able to say it?" (§75). He unpacks this further in a paragraph that is at once cryptic and yet almost poetic.

> Compare *knowing* and *saying*:
>
>> how many feet high Mont Blanc is—
>> how the word "game" is used—
>> how a clarinet sounds.
>
> If you are surprised that one can know something and not be able to say it, you are perhaps thinking of a case like the first. Certainly not of one like the third. (§78)

Knowing *how* to use a word, Wittgenstein suggests, is more like knowing how a clarinet sounds than knowing how many feet high Mont Blanc is. And knowing what a game is—*like learning how to play a game*—is a kind of knowledge that is socially absorbed. It is the sort of knowledge that is caught in community, like the way we learn our first language because we're embedded in a family context. It will be a long time before I master the grammar of my first language (if ever!). Someone can be a competent, even masterful, speaker of English without learning how to articulate the grammar (cf. §31). That's because speaking is more know-*how* than know-*what*. And Wittgenstein believes that vast reservoirs of know-how are the condition of possibility for engaging in the know-what game of definition and analysis. It is our mastery of blurred concepts that makes it possible for us, for certain purposes, to stipulate sharper, defined concepts. But Wittgenstein cautions against thinking such clarity is either fundamental or a universal ideal. There are all sorts of instances in which rigidity will actually detract from usefulness (§79).

It is in this way, and for this reason, that Wittgenstein relativizes the claims of logic without simply rejecting them. What he rejects, we might say, is a kind of logical fundamentalism. The analytic tradition that Wittgenstein is pressing up against has a tendency to see logic as an "ideal language" that is then taken to be the norm for *all* languages, even if only in an aspirational sense. In this context he is riffing on F. P. Ramsey's claim that logic is a "normative science" (§81), but he's also responding to his own earlier claims in the *Tractatus*. Wittgenstein grants that we might see logic as just such an "ideal" language. But then "the most that can be said is that we *construct* ideal languages. But here the word 'ideal' is liable to mislead, for it sounds as if these languages were better, more perfect than our everyday language; and as if it took the logician to shew people at last what a proper sentence looked like" (§81). But logic is not as "sublime" as we've been told: "For there seemed to pertain to logic a peculiar depth—a universal significance. Logic lay, it seemed, at the bottom of all the sciences. For logical investigation explores the nature of all things. It seeks to see to the bottom of things and is not meant to concern itself with whether what actually happens is this or that" (§89). In short, logic is a "language" that is eviscerated of contingency and particularity. Of course, that is a game you can play, Wittgenstein says; but let's not confuse this with an account of how we embodied, finite, contingent, dependent creatures make our way in the world.[18]

Instead he cites Augustine's famous claim from the *Confessions*: "What then is time? Provided that no one asks me, I know. If I want to explain it to an inquirer, I do not know."[19] This is the kind of thing we know but can't say; so it's also the kind of knowledge that can't be made sense of in the language of logic. Thus Wittgenstein concludes on a note of caution that borders on the mystical: "Something that we know when no one asks us, but no longer know when we are supposed to give an account of it, is something that we need to *remind* ourselves of. (And it is obviously something of which for some reason it is difficult to remind oneself.)" (§89).

18. And, in fact, our "clarification" is always selective. This is why I often find myself frustrated, for example, by the project of "analytic theology," which takes itself to be clearing up all the muddled fuzziness of theology (as practiced by theologians) by bringing the (alleged) conceptual clarity of philosophical analysis to bear on our theological claims. (Philosophers generally think that if you want anything done well, get a philosopher to do it.) But as I read the emerging literature in "analytic theology," I'm always struck by just what counts as clarification. Certainly they home in on specific terms and apply logical analysis in order to refine how those terms relate to each other. But in the process, I'm always amazed at what terms remain unclarified and assumed. We all work with fuzziness and blurred concepts. We just pick *which* to leave "fuzzy."

19. Wittgenstein cites the Latin of the *Confessions*. I have cited Henry Chadwick's translation (Oxford: Oxford University Press, 1991), 11.14.17.

Picturing "Meaning as Use" in *Lars and the Real Girl*

Wittgenstein's "pragmatism" is a philosophy of contingency, attentive and attuned to the social structures of dependence that are the webs within which our world "means" something. As such, I believe that it can also serve as a philosophy of creaturehood, one that gets at the knotty issues at the intersection of language, meaning, and reality. If Wittgenstein's theory can be summarized in the slogan "meaning is use," it's crucial that we hear the fundamental claim *behind* that account: that meaning and knowledge are ineluctably *social* and communal. Our knowing the "real" is bound up with—and inextricably linked to—the social fabric(s) into which we are woven. Community is the condition of possibility for meaning, even for "reality," in a sense. And much of our ability to know the world is more a kind of know-*how*, a bearing we bring to the world, a feel for the world that we have learned from others. (Usually at this point in my course someone brings up the counterexample of feral children![20]) Just to know the world is to be indebted to a community of practice. Our knowing is dependent upon—and relative to—those communities of practice. We are all like brickies who have learned to play a game on the job. (Your knowledge is already relative to relatives!)

I've been trying to suggest that this is not some radical, naturalistic thesis. Wittgenstein's pragmatist account of "meaning as use" is not a prelude to atheism. To the contrary, I think it is precisely the conclusion we should come to if we are attentive to the conditions of creaturehood. If Augustine could draw on the "loot" of Plato, then I'm suggesting that, as Christian philosophers, we can draw on the "loot" of Wittgenstein's pragmatism as a kind of wake-up call to finitude and creaturehood—even if that means *un*learning some acquired habits that have tied us to the rhetoric of realism and representation. But perhaps it would be helpful to try to "picture" this thesis.

I think we find just such a picture in the quirky film *Lars and the Real Girl*. In this story we encounter a know-how that was operative, a communal understanding that enabled a community

---

20. So I was tickled to see that George Lindbeck also alludes to the "wolf children" that are the exception that proves the rule! See Lindbeck, *The Nature of Doctrine: Religion and Theology in a Postliberal Age* (Philadelphia: Westminster, 1984), 34.

to make sense of what was incredible. Some of you are probably familiar with the movie. Set in the bleak cold of a Minnesota winter, the story revolves around Lars Lindstrom—a broken young man in a culture that is not given to articulating emotion or processing trauma. When we meet Lars, he is twenty-seven years old—a kind, gentle young man, and yet profoundly lonely and isolated. He is literally untouchable: he wears layers and layers of clothing in order to avoid any sort of human contact because such contact is physically painful for him.

We slowly learn why this might be: his mother died while giving birth to him. In the wake of this tragedy, his father was a shell of himself and unable to really care for Lars. And his older brother, Gus, scared to confront any of this, left the house as soon as he could. When Gus and his new wife, Karin, return to the family home after their father's death, Lars is displaced to the garage.

No one is really aware of the depth of Lars's brokenness until the story takes a surprising turn. Through machinations that I won't go into here, let's just say that Lars acquires an odd companion: he orders a "doll" of sorts, a kind of mannequin created for, shall we say, "amorous" purposes—though Lars is really just looking for a friend. (The very fact that such artifacts exist in our world is itself a testament to the sad disordering of the social goods of creation.) And so Lars comes to Gus and Karin's door to announce that he has a visitor. Can they come over for dinner? he asks. Excited to see Lars making a connection, Karin and Gus jump at the chance to encourage this relationship.

You can imagine the look on their faces when Lars carries Bianca into their living room. The stunned silence is deafening. Lars has invented an entire backstory for Bianca: she is a missionary, raised by nuns, now on sabbatical (not the usual back story for dolls of this sort!). Indeed, Bianca told him that God made her to help people.

Poor Gus and Karin don't know how to process this. Well, actually, Gus has an immediate diagnosis: "He's crazy! What are we going to do?!" Eventually, they bring him to see the local physician, Dagmar, who encourages them to help Lars through his delusion by receiving Bianca *as human*—by treating her as Lars sees her: as *real*. Gus can hardly believe this. "No, no, no, no . . . ," he mutters, there's no way he can do that. They have to, the doctor counsels. "But everyone's going to laugh at him," Gus protests.

"And you," Dagmar warns him. She wants him to understand what he's signing up for.

You might say that Dagmar is pressing them to play a whole new game: a game in which Bianca is *real*, a language-game in which an inanimate doll is *meant* as the cherished girlfriend of Lars. But in fact it turns out they've been practicing for this game all along because they have been trained as a community of love. At the heart of this story is one of the most beautiful pictures of the church that you'll ever see on the screen. Indeed, the film opens in a tiny Lutheran church where we see Lars listening attentively to the sermon. And in this opening scene we hear the pastor exhort this humble, nondescript band of Jesus followers: "We need never ask, 'Lord, what should I do?' because the Lord has *told* us what to do: 'Love one another.' That, my friends, is the one true law." This foreshadows the kind of community into which Bianca will arrive. It's also part of the communal "training" that has created a context in which Bianca will be loved, because Lars is loved. Love *means* the world here, and truth shouldn't be narrowly circumscribed by empirical concerns about correspondence.

The rubber hits the road when Gus and Karin attend a vestry meeting to explain their situation. They want to receive Bianca *as* human, and they want the congregation to do the same. Despite a few grumpy protests, in fact it is love that wins the day: of course Bianca is welcome in church—which, of course, is just to say that *Lars*, in all his brokenness, is welcome in church. That's not to say that the scene isn't a tad awkward on the following Sunday. There are furtive glances and long, puzzled stares. But this peculiar people image God to Lars and Bianca: with flowers for Bianca, with invitations for the two of them, even with opportunities for Bianca to serve throughout the community. They wash her and dress her and put her to bed. And what's beautiful is that we see signs that they're doing this *even when Lars doesn't know*. What we see, then, is a community in which Bianca is "the real girl."

But, of course, *Bianca's not real!* the realist will protest. This is like a communal delusion. This is social constructionism run amok.

Should we really be worried about correspondence theories of truth here? Does scrupulously policing "the real" really guarantee *truth* in this context? Is "reality" on the side of ontological parsimony, or love? If loving Bianca is wrong, then I don't want to be right. Because in that tiny Minnesota town—the town that is home to Lars and still carries the memory of his mom and dad—loving Bianca is *true*.

In fact, at a crucial point in the movie, when Bianca is taken out for the night to a community event, Lars is having a bit of a "What-about-me?" self-pity party, complaining that Bianca has abandoned him and that nobody cares. "People do whatever they want," Lars whines. "They don't care."

But his sister-in-law Karin loves him enough to also name the truth: "That is just *not true*," she protests. "God! Every person in this town bends over backwards to make Bianca feel at home. . . . Because all these people love *you*. . . . None of this is easy for any of us. But we do it for *you*."

This is the turning point in Lars's story: this is the good news he needed to hear, needed to know, needed to realize. They have loved him toward wholeness by being the sort of peculiar people who could welcome the unbelievable. They have enacted the truth in their doing. And Bianca loves them back! In a moving scene at Bianca's funeral (long story!), the quiet country pastor testifies: "From her wheelchair, Bianca reached out and touched us all in ways we could never have imagined. . . . She was a lesson in courage. And Bianca loved us all, especially Lars. Especially him."

As a community with a kind of know-how that makes no sense if you articulate it in propositions and package it as a syllogism, they have *meant* Bianca as "the real girl" *in order to* love Lars and be that people who do what Jesus would do. Meaning *as use* is always relative to *an end*, a goal. Since love is the *telos* of this community of practice, the ultimate context in which they make sense of the world, they *mean* Bianca *as* the real girl.

When I first saw this movie I couldn't stop thinking about a passage from Paul's first letter to the Corinthians (1:26–29).

> Consider your own call, brothers and sisters: not many of you were wise by human standards, not many were powerful, not many were of noble birth. But God chose what is foolish in the world to shame the wise; God chose what is weak in the world to shame the strong; God chose what is low and despised in the world, *things that are not*, to reduce to nothing things that are, so that no one might boast in the presence of God.

God's economy of "reality" does not seem to map neatly onto our fetish for "realism." Instead, God uses the "are nots" to redeem the world. He who created out of nothing uses the "are nots" of this world to *recall* creation into being. And so in this little nondescript congregation in a nondescript town, the people of God love Bianca *as human* in order to love Lars into human wholeness. Stanley Hauerwas once remarked: "We do not see reality by just opening our eyes."[21] The real is constructed as much as it is discovered; it is made as much as it is recognized.[22] And to see the real—to *make* the real—requires the right training. In *Lars and the Real Girl* we see a community trained to make love, you might say—to make the world in and by love.

Learning How to Use the World: Augustine the Relativist

What we see pictured in *Lars and the Real Girl* is something like a Christian rendition of Wittgenstein's thesis: meaning is use, constituted by a community, and when that community is defined by *love*, then the world *means* something different.[23] It is nothing short of a reconfiguration of "the real." "Meaning as use" just means that meaning is always indexed to an *end*, a *telos*; and we (only) become oriented to a *telos* through our immersion in a social body, a community of practice that teaches us how to use the world.

If this sounds like some radical, postmodern thesis, it's actually quite ancient. It's at least as old as St. Augustine. So in order to "take Wittgenstein to church," how about we bring him to visit the bishop?

I would suggest Wittgenstein's intuition was anticipated by Augustine's philosophy of language as laid out in *De doctrina christiana*.[24] Despite how this title is sometimes translated, *De doctrina*

---

21. Stanley Hauerwas, *Vision and Virtue: Essays in Christian Ethical Reflection* (Notre Dame, IN: University of Notre Dame Press, 1986), 36.

22. This has implications for the prospects of any "natural theology," which we will discuss in chaps. 3 and 4 below. Hauerwas teases out similar implications in *With the Grain of the Universe: The Church's Witness and Natural Theology* (Grand Rapids: Brazos, 2001).

23. Actually, Augustine would say it is not a question of *whether* our community loves, but *what* they love (in *City of God* 19.24–26).

24. Sometimes mistranslated as *On Christian Doctrine*, in fact it is better translated as *On Christian Teaching*, or, as Edmund Hill does, *Teaching Christianity*,

is not a summary of Christian *doctrine*; instead, it is a manual for Christian *teaching*. As a bishop, Augustine was responsible for training the preachers in his diocese. And as a former rhetorician himself, he had strong opinions on the subject. So *Teaching Christianity* is his manual for preachers, amounting to a Christian rhetoric. Given the medium of the preacher's task, *De doctrina* is also Augustine's mature articulation of a philosophy of language.[25] But as we'll see, his philosophy of language is bound up with his ontology, his philosophy of reality.

Interestingly, Wittgenstein's *Philosophical Investigations* actually opens with a long quotation from Augustine—not from *De doctrina*, but from book 1 of his *Confessions*, which includes a section on language.

> When they (my elders) named some object, and accordingly moved towards something, I saw this and I grasped that the thing was called by the sound they uttered when they meant to point it out. Their intention was shewn by their bodily movements, as it were the natural language of all peoples: the expression of the face, the play of the eyes, the movement of other parts of the body, and the tone of voice which expresses our state of mind in seeking, having, rejecting, or avoiding something. Thus, as I heard words repeatedly used in their proper places in various sentences, I gradually learnt to understand what objects they signified; and after I had trained my mouth to form these signs, I used them to express my own desires.[26]

As you might guess, Augustine makes this cameo appearance in the opening of Wittgenstein's *Investigations* as a poster child for the "picture" theory of language, the representationalist account of language in which every word refers to some thing—precisely the theory that Wittgenstein is rejecting. As he later summarizes Augustine's view, "Augustine describes the learning of human language as if the child came into a strange country and did not understand the language of the country; that is, as if it already had a language, only not this one. Or again: as if the child could

---

The Works of Saint Augustine I/11 (New York: New City Press, 1996); henceforth abbreviated as *DC*.

25. He also deals with philosophy of language in an earlier work, *De magistro*. I have discussed that early work more fully in *Speech and Theology: Language and the Logic of Incarnation*, Radical Orthodoxy Series (New York: Routledge, 2002), 114–49.

26. *Confessions* 1.8, as cited and translated in *PI*, §1.

already *think*, only not yet speak" (§32). The only sort of training in Augustine's account is ostensive: our parents teach us to correlate words with things. In other words, Augustine's picture in the *Confessions* is guilty of the narrow propositionalism that Wittgenstein is rejecting.

So it would seem like a doomed project to now try to argue that Augustine actually anticipates Wittgenstein's account of "meaning as use." But the picture of language and meaning laid out in book 1 of the *Confessions* is quite different from the rich, nuanced account we get in Augustine's later work *Teaching Christianity*. When we look at this later work, I think we'll find something very much akin to Wittgenstein's social account of meaning—but now articulated by a bishop and rooted in biblical convictions.

The Blurry Boundary between "Words" and "Things"

If the picture of language acquisition in the *Confessions* reduces meaning to the correlation of words and things, *De doctrina* makes the distinction between words and things only to immediately complicate it. First the distinction: "All teaching," Augustine tells us, "is either about things or signs; but things are learned about through signs. What I have now called things, though, in the strict sense, are those that are not mentioned in order to signify something, such as wood, a stone, an animal, and other things like that" (*DC* 1.2.2). So he carves up the world into "signs" and "things." Signs are pointers, indicators: they refer (i.e., point) to things. Signs, quite simply, *signify* something else, whereas "things" are not pointers or signifiers. The written marks "t-r-e-e" constitute a *sign* because they point to—and bring to mind—the *thing* that is tall and green. Signs are always instrumental—they point beyond themselves—whereas things are kind of ends in themselves, a stopping point. You go *through* a sign to get to a thing. In this sense, Augustine repeats a classic distinction that is repeated right up through the twentieth century.

However, Augustine immediately complicates the picture. "Things," he tells us, are "not mentioned in order to signify something else"—except when they do! Listen to Augustine's qualifier in context:

What I have now called things . . . in the strict sense are those that are not mentioned in order to signify something, such as wood, a stone, an animal, and other things like that. *Not, however,* that piece of wood which we read of Moses throwing into the bitter water to remove its bitterness; nor that stone which Jacob placed under his head; nor that animal which Abraham sacrificed instead of his son. All these, in fact, are things *in such a way as* also to be signs of other things. (*DC* 1.2.2, emphases added)

Almost as soon as he carved up the world into things and signs, Augustine blurs the distinction by reminding us of a number of "things" in Scripture that actually serve *as* signs, and often signs of Christ. The distinction is destabilized precisely because it begins to seem that just about anything could be a sign.

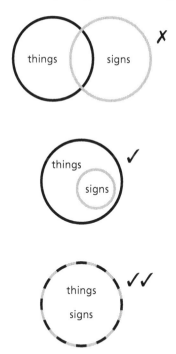

The (in)distinction between "things" and "signs"

Which raises the question: When is a thing a sign? How would you know? If a stone or a tree can be a sign, then it would seem just about *anything* could be a sign. And in fact, for Augustine, because the entire creation is a *sacramentum mundi*, any *thing* is capable of functioning as a *sign*; any thing "can be employed to signify" (*DC* 1.2.2). So the distinction between things and signs is not ontological or metaphysical; it is *functional* and *contextual*. Sign-ness—the sort of meaning that is referential—does not substantially inhere in a certain subset of things; rather, things function *as* signs when they are "taken" as signs by human listeners and readers. It's not that signs are made out of a certain kind of stuff; rather, they are things that are *used* in a certain sort of way. Signs are things that we use.

But Augustine's point is even more radical than that because we still have to answer this question: How and when do you know that a thing is to be *used* as a sign? In other words, how do we learn which things are to be used as signs? Or how do we know *when* to use them as signs? If their sign-ness—their signifying power—is not a metaphysical property but rather a question of function, then even recognizing when a thing should function as a sign (i.e., something to be used) is itself a matter of *use*. Nothing is just "objectively" a sign: things function *as* signs within a community of practice. What the community ultimately teaches me is what to love; and what I love will determine how I use the world.

What's Love Got to Do with It? On "Use" and "Enjoyment"

This is why, immediately after introducing his blurry distinction between signs and things, Augustine makes a second crucial distinction: between "use" (*uti*) and "enjoyment" (*frui*). He introduces it this way: "There are some things which are meant to be enjoyed, others which are meant to be used, yet others which *do* both the enjoying and the using. Things that are to be enjoyed make us happy; things which are to be used help us on our way to happiness (*DC* 1.3.3)."

You'll notice that this distinction sort of parallels the distinction between signs and things. Like signs, some things we *use* for other ends—namely, enjoyment (or happiness or blessedness or what Aristotle would call *eudaimonia*). Things that we enjoy are ends in themselves, ultimate goods. In fact Augustine says that the things we *enjoy* are the things we *love*: "Enjoyment, after all, consists in clinging to something lovingly for its own sake, while use consists in referring [note the sign-like language] what has come your way to what your love aims at obtaining, provided, that is, it *deserves* to be loved" (*DC* 1.4.4, emphasis added). What you love is what you enjoy; and what you enjoy is what you love—what you treat as ultimate, what you treat as an end in itself.

So some things we use, others we love, which invites the question: Which are which?! How can we know the difference? Here Augustine points out that we human beings are unique creatures because we inhabit an ambiguous "between" space: we are those "things" who *do* both enjoying and using. "We ourselves," he says, "both enjoy and use things, and find ourselves in the middle, in a position to choose which to do" (1.4.4). And if we get this wrong, we frustrate our happiness. "So if we wish to enjoy things that are *meant* to be used, we are impeding our own progress, and sometimes are also deflected from our course, because we are thereby delayed in obtaining what we should be enjoying, or turned back from it altogether, blocked by our love for inferior things" (1.4.4, emphasis added). Augustine uses a travel metaphor to illustrate the point: we *use* a ship to get to our destination, which is our *end*, the location of our enjoyment. But if we end up treating the ship as an end in itself, *enjoying* it rather than *using* it, we'll never get to our destination. We fall in love with the conveyance rather than enjoying the blessings of the destination. In Augustine's "prodigal" version of the story, this means we never get home.

There is a crucial assumption in Augustine's analysis that we need to highlight: it is embedded in the normative language he employs in this discussion. Notice that some things are *meant* to be used, while other things *deserve* to be loved; some things are described as *inferior*, whereas other things are seen as *ultimate* goods. Some things *ought* to be used; other things *ought* to be enjoyed. This is language that is both *normative* and (because of that) *evaluative*. Because there are better and worse things, higher and lower goods, there are corresponding obligations for us creatures in this "between" space: we ought to enjoy the higher and use the lower; we ought to treat inferior things as "signs" that refer us to ultimate things that are ends-in-themselves to be enjoyed. This order of evaluation and obligation is what Augustine calls the *ordo amoris*, the right order of love. And once again, the distinction is a bit destabilized when he unpacks the right order of use/enjoyment because ultimately, the "things . . . that are to be enjoyed are the Father and the Son and the Holy Spirit, in fact the Trinity, one supreme thing, and one which is shared in common by all who enjoy it" (1.5.5). But then Augustine immediately catches himself: "*if*, that is to say, it is a thing, and not the cause of all things; *if* indeed it is a cause. It is not easy, after all, to find any name that will really fit such transcendent majesty" (1.5.5).

The Triune God is that thing above all things—the source of everything who is beyond "thing"-ness—which we are made to enjoy, made to love. When our love is ordered to this end, then the whole of creation becomes a sign, referring us beyond it to the Creator. And when our love is so ordered, we can also delight *in creation* in a sense. Augustine puts it this way: "When something that is loved is available to you, delight is also bound to accompany it; but if you pass through this and refer it to that end where you are to remain permanently, you are really using it, and are said by a figure of speech, and not in the proper sense of the word, to enjoy it" (1.33.37). You might think of this as a distinction between capital-*E* and small-*e* enjoyment: if our love is so ordered that we find our ultimate Enjoyment in the Triune Creator, then we will be able to use creation in such a way that it can be small-*e* enjoyed, received as a gift that leads us to the Giver.[27] If we don't—if our love is disordered and we Enjoy the creation rather than the Creator—then creation becomes an idol rather than an icon, a "thing" instead of a "sign."

The analogy and parallel has now come full circle. What makes a thing a sign is *how* we "use" it; the distinction between things and signs is functional, not ontological. So, similarly, whether creation functions as a thing or a sign of the Creator is a matter of *how* we relate to it—a matter of *how* we love. Whether creation

27. Augustine suggests a similar kind of distinction between what we might call capital-*L* and small-*l* love: "This we should be making use of with a certain love and delight that is not, so to say, permanently settled in, but transitory, rather, and causal, like love and delight in a road, or in vehicles, or any other tools and gadgets you like, or if you can think of any better way of putting it, so that we love the means by which we are being carried along, on account of the goal to which we are being carried" (1.35.39). So I could be said to love that path to Grantchester because I Love the tea garden that lies at the end of the path; I enjoy the stroll to Grantchester as part of the experience of ultimately Enjoying tea on the River Cam (in the same garden where Wittgenstein did the same!).

functions as a sign *depends* on what we do with it. And yet there is also a normative dynamic here: Augustine clearly stipulates that we *ought* to use creation, not enjoy it. There is a right order of love to which we should conform.

Which again raises the question, *How do we know this?* What is the basis for this "right order of love"? How do we come to know that this is the right order of love? How do we know that the Trinity is the *telos* of human happiness? How do we know this "order" by which we are to evaluate everything? Is this "objectively" true of creation? Is it self-evident? And if so, then why do some people seem to have a very different "read" on this world?

Augustine's answer here is appropriately complicated. First, he recognizes that a "right order" of love must be relative to some criteria of evaluation. The very notion of "right order" is inherently normative. So "living a just and holy life requires one to be capable of an objective and impartial evaluation of things; to love things, that is to say, in the right order, so that you do not love what is not to be loved, or fail to love what is to be loved, or have a greater love for what should be loved less," and so on (*DC* 1.27.28). We are *meant* to love the Triune God above all, and that ultimate love (enjoyment) is meant to order all of our penultimate attachments. Augustine affirms that this is the way creation is designed: we might say that ontologically this order is a feature of the cosmos created by the Triune God.

However, the *recognition* of that fact—indeed, the very ability to know the Triune God and hence the order of love he commands—is dependent upon the grace of revelation unfolded in the Scriptures and proclaimed by the church.[28] The use/enjoyment distinction is not "objective" in the sense that it can be just "read off" the world before us. The very distinction between use and enjoyment—the order of love—is *relative to* a story, the story revealed in the Scriptures, proclaimed in the gospel, and handed down to us in the body of Christ. Even when we take the distinction to be *true*, receiving

28. We have a tendency to think that relativism precludes norms; or that normative language must be "absolute." But I think Augustine's account here challenges that picture, highlighting that, in fact, our norms are relative to the story/community of practice in which we are immersed. Augustine obviously thinks these norms inhere in the universe—they really are features of the cosmos. But they are only known in and through our immersion in that community of practice that receives and hands down the Word of God.

this as the "true story of the whole world," we are always already dependent upon this social context of reception and proclamation, this community of practice that teaches us how to *mean* the world as a gift. Like that Minnesota town in *Lars and the Real Girl*, it is a community of practice that equips us with the know-how to see "the real" for what it is. In this sense, meaning is irreducibly social.

And God is neither surprised by nor allergic to this. Instead, in the gracious condescension of his incarnational being, God's revelation meets us *in* and *under* these social conditions of meaning. God's revelation meets us in these conditions of contingency and dependence. That's why the Triune God doesn't just send us an "objective" Word; he sends his Son who, upon his ascension, imparts the Spirit who gives birth to a community of practice to enable us to read his world. Our revealing Creator is not just incarnational; he is pentecostal. He doesn't just send us a message; he enfolds us into his body. And that body is the community of practice in which we learn to mean the world—the context in which we learn what the world is *for*. Our seeing the world as a gift to be used is relative to our immersion in the Story in which that makes sense. The church is the language-game in which we learn to read the world aright. If there is no salvation outside the church, we might also say that there is no use/enjoyment distinction outside the church either. The church is that "conventional" community in which the Spirit trains us to know the real world. But that immersion in the conventions of a community of practice is an essential feature of such a Spirit-ed "realism," a realism without representation.

3

Who's Afraid of Contingency?

Owning Up to Our Creaturehood with Rorty

Richard Rorty is a philosopher that realists love to hate (which means, *mutatis mutandis*, he's a philosopher that Christian philosophers also love to hate). The dense, hyphenated forests of Heidegger's language are too puzzling to be bothered with; and the maddening play of Derrida's French acrobatics is mystifying and frustrating; so when analytic philosophers look around for an "anti-realist" whipping boy and poster child of all that is wrong with postmodernism, they usually target Richard Rorty. Educated at the University of Chicago and Yale, tenured as a philosopher at Princeton, Rorty spoke their language. His accessible prose and facility with Quine and Sellars made him *sound* like one of their own. But then he would say the most ludicrous, provocative things. For example, we've already encountered Alvin Plantinga's perplexed dismissal of Rorty's claim that "truth is what your peers will let you get away with saying." As Plantinga concluded, this seems clearly antithetical to any claim to objective truth, and thus equally antithetical to Christian faith.

But as I hope to show, when we understand the *argument* that surrounds this jarring claim, we will find that, not only is Rorty's pragmatism not essentially antithetical to Christian faith, but to the contrary, his account of social justification—extending key insights of Wittgenstein—amounts to a philosophy of creature-hood that ought to be embraced by Christians.[1] I'm not trying to blunt or domesticate the radicality of his claim; rather, my goal is to feel the full force of Rorty's critique of "realism" in order to then critically reconsider our Christian philosophical assumptions. If we go *through* Rorty's critique, rather than merely dismissing it or deflecting it, I believe we might emerge with a Christian philo-sophical account of contingency that befits our status as creatures. In that sense, Rorty's pragmatism might be more an ally than an enemy of an integral Christian philosophy.

Shaking the Foundations: Philosophy's Bad Habits and Pseudoproblems

While Rorty built a significant corpus over his career, I will simply attend to the critical argument in his now-classic work *Philosophy and the Mirror of Nature*.[2] This was the work that made Richard Rorty the "Rorty" who would so often be invoked to say shocking things. It is a work that is both historical and constructive, telling a different story about philosophy in order to philosophize differently. Rorty's relationship to—and critique of—the history of philosophy is essential to his argument in *Philosophy and the Mirror of Nature*. Indeed, the story he has to tell (which takes up the first two-thirds of the book) *is* his "method," in a sense. There are some who be-come easily frustrated with this sort of "forest-rather-than-trees"

1. This obviously means that Rorty's own conclusions about religion—and Chris-tianity in particular—are not entailed by his pragmatist account of knowledge. Indeed, to the contrary, Rorty's nonfoundationalism should have undercut his dismissal of religion. See, for example, Nicholas Wolterstorff's critique of Rorty on this point in "An Engagement with Rorty," *Journal of Religious Ethics* 31 (2003): 129–39. For a (concessionary) response, see Richard Rorty, "Religion in the Public Square: A Re-consideration," *Journal of Religious Ethics* 31 (2003): 141–49.

2. Richard Rorty, *Philosophy and the Mirror of Nature* (Princeton: Princeton University Press, 1979); henceforth abbreviated as *PM*. For a more comprehensive introduction to Rorty's work as a whole, see Ronald Kuipers's excellent, concise volume *Richard Rorty*, Bloomsbury Contemporary American Thinkers (London: Bloomsbury, 2013). Readers who want to follow up within Rorty's corpus should dive into *Contingency, Irony, and Solidarity* (New York: Cambridge University Press, 1989), though Rorty's later collection *Philosophy and Social Hope* (New York: Penguin, 1999) might provide a retrospective introduction.

approach. They prefer to spend their time analyzing trees—and not even just that: they'd rather be analyzing the bark, or the rings, or the leaves of one tree. The game of professional philosophy—and the rat race that is the "tenure track"—encourages philosophers to keep their heads down and plow away at tree analysis, and to think that anyone who is a "serious" or "rigorous" philosopher will devote themselves to tree analysis. But would you want those folks to be in charge of drawing a map of the forest? Would you want to ask them how to get back to camp? What if these are the wrong trees?

If we run with this metaphor, Rorty is interested in remapping the forest because he thinks a lot of philosophers have mistakenly set to work on certain trees because they've inherited a bad directive, as it were. Or we might say that, according to Rorty's story, these philosophers are devoting their analytic labor to "fake plastic trees" (to paraphrase Radiohead). As a mapmaker, Rorty's project is to zoom out and ask, What sort of a forest is this? What are we doing here? And why? Is *this* what philosophy should be worried about? In order to raise these big questions, he needs to tell a story at a "meta-" level.

Now some mistakenly think that if we're dealing with a story, then we're *not* getting an "argument." But I think that's a false dichotomy and betrays a narrow imagination about what counts as an argument. Rorty is very much trying to offer an argument: he's taking a position, offering evidence, and trying to persuade us. But the argument itself is, we might say, "narratival" in form. He's asking, "How did we get here?" and the answer to that question is inevitably a story—a hi*story* of modern philosophy. So let's get a plot summary before attending to the specifics.

For Rorty, the very fact that philosophy became a "discipline" was sort of the beginning of the end. As a professional discipline, philosophy takes *knowledge* to be its subject and specialty (a narrow fixation that would have surprised Plato or Cicero). In particular, professional philosophy is concerned with issues of *legitimation* or *justification*: What do we know, how do we know it, and who says? "Philosophy as a discipline thus sees itself as the attempt to underwrite or debunk claims to knowledge made by science, morality, art, or religion" (*PM*, 3). In this way, philosophy also sets itself up as the arbiter of *culture*, sort of the border patrol of meaning and significance. If you make any claims, you have to report to the philosophers, show them your papers (evidence), and they'll decide whether to let you into the country called "rationality." But philosophy can only police culture in this way because it reduces culture *to* "knowledge." When you're an epistemologist, everything is a proposition. And insofar as modern philosophy reduces knowledge to *representation* (more specifically, the ability of the mind to represent what is "outside" the mind), philosophy thus evaluates different sectors of culture on their ability to represent reality: some do this well (science), some less well (art, literature?), some not at all (religion, morality?).

Rorty sees this configuration of philosophy's task and field as entirely contingent, tracing it back to important shifts in the seventeenth century (Locke, Descartes), culminating in the Kantian paradigm of the eighteenth century—which is "completed" as it were in the various Neokantianisms of the twentieth century (whether analytic or continental) that tried to "ground" all sorts of things.[3] On this model, philosophy "is a tribunal of pure reason, upholding or denying the claims of the rest of culture" (*PM*, 4). Here Rorty makes an interesting observation: conceived in this way, philosophy "became, for intellectuals, a substitute for religion" insofar as it functioned as a "final vocabulary," "the area of culture where one touched bottom" (4). But then a funny thing happened on the way to secularization: when secularism gradually triumphed, philosophy was no longer needed as a cultural antidote to superstition—which left it with little cultural relevance. While various streams continued their work of "grounding" culture, "the attempts of both analytic philosophers and phenomenologists to 'ground' this and 'criticize' that were shrugged off by those whose activities were purportedly being grounded or criticized" (5). The result was the cultural marginalization of philosophy, which is why the profession is now largely irrelevant to wider public discourse. And yet these sorts of philosophical worries gradually became sedimented in popular consciousness so that now everyone is worried about "correspondence." Our "folk" epistemologies—the unstated working assumptions we make about knowledge—have

---

3. Rorty's pragmatism is, in some ways, more radical than the phenomenological projects of Heidegger and Derrida precisely because the latter still seem to retain some version of this "representationalist" paradigm. This is why deconstruction ends in "anti-realist" skepticism, whereas pragmatism rejects the representationalist paradigm altogether and thus doesn't have to choose between realism or anti-realism.

trickled down from Descartes and Locke. So now parishioners in the pew will raise questions that first worried Descartes. We're all fretting skeptics now.

But this direction for philosophy was *contingent*. It could have gone otherwise. So the proper response to this ill-conceived project, Rorty suggests, is not a tit-for-tat response to the proposals of Descartes, Locke, or Kant. That would be akin to repairing the dance floor on the Titanic. Instead, philosophy needs to refuse the hand it's been (contingently) dealt. To do so, Rorty turns to the work of his therapeutic trinity: Wittgenstein, Heidegger, and Dewey. In their work, philosophy "broke free of the Kantian conception of philosophy as foundational" (5). Rorty sees their projects as "therapeutic" and "edifying" because they are "designed to make the reader *question his own motives for philosophizing*" (5–6, emphasis added). These three refuse the terms of debate as they've been framed. They are "in agreement that the notion of knowledge as accurate representation made possible by special mental processes, and intelligible through a general theory of representations, needs to be abandoned." So it's not that they are offering "*alternative* 'theories of knowledge' or 'philosophies of mind.'" Instead, "they glimpse the possibility of a form of intellectual life in which the vocabulary of philosophical reflection inherited from the seventeenth century would seem as pointless as the thirteenth-century philosophical vocabulary had seemed to the Enlightenment" (6). Their project is not revisionist or reformist, but "revolutionary" (in Thomas Kuhn's terms): they offer us "new maps of the terrain" (7). The project of *Philosophy and the Mirror of Nature*, then, is to survey and summarize these developments and point out the dead-end direction of philosophy in the "Kantian" (foundationalist) tradition.[4]

4. In particular, he will show that the "linguistic turn" in contemporary philosophy actually does nothing to displace philosophy's Kantian habits (*PM*, 8). This is because the linguistic turn is just representationalism by other means. Rorty wants to show that much that traffics under the banner of the "linguistic turn" is not some radical revolution in philosophy; rather, it is a continuation of the Kantian project by other means. While this *seems* like they're being attentive to the empirical contingency of language, in fact they are "transcendentalizing" language *as if* it were not contingent (258)—they attempt to "de-transcendentalize epistemology while nevertheless making it do what we had always hoped it might" (299). In other words, language is seen as a new a priori (266). In this respect, Rorty's critique is very much analogous to Derrida's critique of Plato and Husserl, who both let the seeming "immateriality" of

Ultimately, Rorty sees this modern philosophical project "as an attempt to escape from history" (*PM*, 9). In that sense, Rorty's project is to get philosophy to own up to its—and to *our*—contingency and historicity (9). That will look less like a realist "correspondence theory of truth" and more like a "Deweyan conception of knowledge" in which knowledge is understood as "what we are justified in believing," where justification is understood as a *social* phenomenon "rather than a transaction between 'the knowing subject' and 'reality'" (9). That will mean owning up to the ways in which knowledge is socially constrained and constructed. Rorty will then wed this to a pragmatist understanding of truth, no longer as "accurate representation" but "what it is better for us to believe" (10). "Accurate representation," then, is just an "empty compliment that we pay to those beliefs that are successful in helping us do what we want to do" (10).

Now, there's a legitimate question that can already be posed to Rorty: If his pragmatist account is going to have some purchase, must there not be a sense in which it is *true*? In other words, must he not believe that his account is not arbitrary? Yes, I think so. This hinges on distinguishing what is "contingent" from what is "arbitrary"—two terms that we often mistakenly treat as synonyms. If we make that distinction, we'll see that Rorty can say there is something about our communal finitude that makes his "Deweyan account" have its force without this amounting to a covert "correspondence" claim. Explaining that is the endgame of *Philosophy and the Mirror of Nature*.

The Illusions of Epistemology: Representationalism Revisited

Rorty sets himself up as a philosophical "therapist." Like any good therapy, this requires working through our story. So the first half of *Philosophy and the Mirror of Nature* amounts to putting

---

speech dupe them into thinking that speech was not contingent, material, and conditioned. Following Donald Davidson and the later Hilary Putnam, Rorty points out the materiality and contingency of language—hence its inability to function as this sort of a priori (e.g., 261). In short, "philosophy of language" remains in the thrall of the "Kantian" project of "grounding" knowledge in something that is not game-relative; that is, it remains a "foundationalist" project that refuses the *pragmatist* turn.

philosophy on the couch to coax out its family history since Descartes. Not until we get the story out can we then analyze it and see where wrong turns were made. The beginning of pragmatism's therapy is to help us identify our hang-ups. You might say that, for Rorty, our fixation on realism and our anxieties about correspondence are symptoms of a contingent philosophical neurosis that needs to be *healed*, not satisfied. So his goal is

> to back up the claim (common to Wittgenstein and Dewey) that to think of knowledge which presents a "problem," and about which we ought to have a "theory," is a product of viewing knowledge as an assemblage of representations—a view of knowledge which . . . was a product of the seventeenth century. The moral to be drawn is that if this way of thinking of knowledge is optional, then so is epistemology, and so is philosophy *as* it has understood itself since the middle of the last century. (*PM*, 136)

The "problem" that perplexes philosophy-as-epistemology— "How do we know there is a world outside of our minds?"—is a pseudoproblem we have created, one that has trickled down to the pews, so to speak. And all the solutions we've come up with to stave off the skepticism inherent in the question (realism, the correspondence theory of truth, etc.) are pseudosolutions: they treat the symptoms of a pseudodisease of our own making. Rorty's pragmatism is an etiology of our philosophical neuroses.

So how did we get here? When and where did the disease begin? Rorty has a long, complicated story to tell here, which I can only summarize in a bit of a highlight reel. Here's the condensed version:

- Descartes creates the *field* of epistemology by inventing "the mind."[5] This "inner space" becomes the cinema for "ideas" and "representations" that play on the screen of consciousness as images *of* a world that is "outside" the mind (a "veil of ideas"). The key to certainty is to "ground"

---

5. What Rorty would have to show, of course, is that "the soul" of Plato, Aristotle, and Aquinas is somehow very different from the Cartesian "mind." Germane to this, cf. John Milbank and Catherine Pickstock's emphasis on distinguishing Aquinas's notion of correspondence from modern notions in *Truth in Aquinas* (London: Routledge, 2003), 4–5.

or "found" ideas or representations of the outside in the foundation of the mind itself. Hence it is Descartes's invention of "mind" that also gives rise to the foundationalist project—namely, securing our knowledge of the "outside" in *something* "inside."[6]

- Locke picks up the Cartesian model and starts fretting about the *mechanics* of mind—just how these ideas and representations "hook up" with and "correspond" to "reality." At this point philosophy just becomes epistemology oriented by a first and basic question: "How is our knowledge possible?"[7] The mind is a tablet on which impressions are inscribed, or a mirror that reflects nature. However, Locke's own answer to this question (empiricism) wasn't characterized by the security of Cartesian certainty (spawning different responses in Hume and Reid).

- Enter Kant who "put philosophy 'on the secure path of science' by putting outer space inside inner space (the space of the constituting activity of the transcendental ego) and then claiming Cartesian certainty about the inner for the laws of what had previously been thought to be outer" (137). "Only Thought Relates" (147) is Kant's maxim—"there are no 'qualified things'—no objects—prior to the 'constitutive action of the mind'" (147). An object is always the result or product of *synthesis*. In other words, since we "constitute" the objects we know, and our ideas are certain, we can be certain about what we constitute.

So we're all Kantians now, even if we spend our time railing against Kant. All subsequent professional philosophy—and not a little of our "folk" philosophizing—will accept this paradigm, even if a lot of energy is spent fighting about the details. The epistemological language-game is the lingua franca of philosophy (and it has trickled down as the language of nonphilosophers too; see,

6. This is why some who reject "classic" foundationalism are still "foundationalist" insofar as they accept the inside/outside distinction and are looking to *ground* our knowledge of the outside.

7. Rorty notes that the history of philosophy gets rewritten, retroactively, after this shift (*PM*, 132–33)—as if Plato and Aristotle and Aquinas were worrying about the same problem.

for example, popular apologetics programs). Philosophy is a quest for the holy grail of "justified true belief." But it was the inside/outside invention that set us out on that quest.

In the process, philosophy takes as "given" what is contingent. What epistemology takes as "given"—as what we "find" when we investigate our "experience"—is in fact *put* there by our training in the epistemology language-game: what we "find" is what we've been trained to see. You have to have been inculcated in this game to "see" things in this way. And once you have been assimilated to this game, it's no longer a game: it's just "the way things are," the "facts of the matter," "reality." The metaphors of tablets and mirrors cease to be metaphorical—which is just to say that we forget the very human and social matrix that gave birth to this account (*PM*, 159).

So we live in what Rorty calls the "neo-Kantian consensus" that "appears as the end-product of an original wish to substitute *confrontation* for *conversation* as the determinant of our belief" (*PM*, 163). In other words, the social web of our knowing drops away, and instead we adopt a working picture of knowledge as atomistic, isolated, interiorized "minds" who are *confronted* by an "external world." For reasons we've already seen in Wittgenstein, Rorty thinks this "representationalist" picture forgets its own contingency. More importantly, it papers over the social character of our knowing. So his project is not to jettison truth or rationality as such, but rather to recover and appreciate the significance of our contingency and dependence, our finitude and our sociality.

Thus Rorty will emphasize the *conversational* nature of our knowledge, and we do well to see this as an extension of Wittgenstein's "meaning as use." "If," Rorty says,

> we think of "rational certainty" as a matter of victory in argument rather than of relation to an object known, we shall look toward our interlocutors rather than to our faculties for the explanation of the phenomenon. If we think of our certainty about the Pythagorean Theorem as our confidence, based on experience with arguments on such matters, that nobody will find an objection to the premises from which we infer it, then we shall not seek to explain it by the relation of reason to triangularity. Our certainty will be a matter of

conversation between persons, rather than a matter of interaction with nonhuman reality. (*PM*, 156–57)[8]

Our claims to knowledge are social and cultural artifacts, and the criteria for their evaluation is equally social and cultural. Here Rorty (like Brandom after him) is extending Wilfrid Sellars's key insight: that we creatures who "know" inhabit "the logical space of reasons"; we are not just subject to a causal relation to objects (*PM*, 157). Our knowledge, one might say, is cultural, not merely natural.[9] So knowledge is more a matter of conversation than of mere confrontation. Making sense of the implications of this is where we turn next.

Beyond Representation: Or, Epistemology as Ethnography

In Rorty's ongoing narrative, the therapeutic trinity of Wittgenstein, Dewey, and Heidegger are privileged as paradigm breakers. But he also sees Quine and Sellars as pointing out chinks in epistemology's armor. But what is it that they all are ultimately contesting? According to Rorty, they call into question the assumption that we can locate some "privileged representations" that function as the ground or "foundation" for knowing (*PM*, 170). Such privileged representations would constitute a kind of *immediacy* (174), a "Mirror of Nature" (170), which are taken as if they were the "*premises* from which our knowledge of other entities is normally inferred" (177). Questioning this picture echoes Wittgenstein's refusal to root meaning in some "interiority."

8. Given that this claim is provocative enough, I wish Rorty was a little more careful. Because when he says that it is a matter of conversation "*rather than* a matter of interaction with nonhuman reality," he has set up a dichotomy that I don't think he sustains later (as we'll see). It's not that "nonhuman reality" is completely irrelevant to the case. Here he is just emphasizing that what makes our knowledge "rational" is as much, and perhaps more fundamentally, a matter of conversation than of "interaction." If he had said "correspondence" rather than "interaction," then the dichotomy would be correct. I don't think his account denies "interaction" per se.

9. In response to critics like Brandom and Bjørn Ramberg, Rorty was later even more explicit about this and retreated from his earlier attempts to reduce objectivity to intersubjectivity. For a helpful, succinct discussion of these issues, see Kuipers, *Richard Rorty*, chap. 5.

Rorty describes their alternative in several different ways: as a "holism" (170, 174); as an account of truth/knowledge/justification that is rooted in social practice rather than privileged representations; as a model where justification is a matter of *conversation* (170–71); and as an "epistemological behaviorism" as opposed to an algorithm of knowledge (174–75, 182). Unpacking these different angles on the alternative might help fill out the picture of what Rorty is suggesting.

This conversational account of knowledge is "holistic" in the sense that, instead of reducing knowledge to discrete correlations between words and things or internal minds and external worlds (the "Mirror of Nature"), knowledge is seen as an *accomplishment* that requires immersion in—and indebtedness to—a web of social practices. Knowledge is a complex, social accomplishment that includes all the sort of know-*how* that can't be articulated in propositions or summarized as "beliefs." "We understand knowledge when we understand the social justification of belief, and thus have no need to view it as accuracy of representation" (*PM*, 170).

Appreciating knowledge as a social accomplishment primes us to then recognize that the "justification" of our knowledge is rooted in that web of social interaction. Justification is not a matter of a special relation between ideas (or words) and objects, but of conversation, of social practice. Epistemology, then, will no longer be the "science" that secures the foundational correlation between mental representations and external reality. Instead, if something like "epistemology" is going to continue, it would be more a matter of ethnography—a philosophical distillation of our social practices of justification. It will be less a physics of knowledge and more like a sociology of knowledge.[10] This is why Rorty describes his pragmatist account as an "epistemological behaviorism" that explains rationality and epistemic authority by reference to "what society lets us say" (*PM*, 174). ("Society" here is the analogue of Wittgenstein's community of practice. This is less some appeal to a national tribunal and more a way of talking about a social context like the bricklayers engaged in a common project.)

10. Which makes Neil Gross's sociological approach to Rorty's own story all the more interesting. See Gross, *Richard Rorty: The Making of an American Philosopher* (Chicago: University of Chicago Press, 2008).

Philosophy as the "study of human knowledge," then, would just be "the study of certain ways in which human beings interact" rather than looking to secure or ground knowledge on some "ontological foundation."[11] If we want to analyze and make sense of "S knows that p," we do better to see that as "a remark about the status of S's report among his peers" than to take it "as a remark about the relation between subject and object, between nature and its mirror" (PM, 175). This will feel like a "deflationary" account of knowledge and truth *only if* you're holding out for a foundationalist explanation. But Rorty isn't just saying that's impossible (which would be a merely skeptical conclusion); he's saying we should stop *wanting* that because it reduces us to merely passive mirrors and fails to appreciate that knowledge is a human, social accomplishment.

Rorty is not giving up on "truth"; he is offering therapy to try to get us off our need for truth-as-correspondence. It's like Descartes and Locke were pushers who got us hooked on the drug of representation, and now we all need our correspondence fix. In that context, Rorty is a rehab counselor, not offering new drugs but trying to stem the addiction and desire. "To be a behaviorist in the large sense in which Sellars and Quine are," Rorty says, "is not to offer reductionist analysis, but to refuse to attempt a certain sort of explanation" (PM, 176). As Wittgenstein would put it, sometimes wisdom is knowing when to stop asking some questions. So rather than looking to ground truth as correspondence, we do better to see truth as "warranted assertability"—truth as "what our peers will, *ceteris paribus*, let us get away with saying" (176). Truth, then, is a matter of "what it is good for us to believe" rather than the metaphysical acrobatics of "contact with reality."

When epistemology makes this turn—to a consideration of human social practices—then it will have to be more attuned to the contingency and particularity of human finitude, to the conditions of creaturehood. Knowledge is only relevant for those creatures who can come under *rules*. And

we can only come under epistemic rules when we have entered the community where the game governed by these rules is played.

11. As we will see below, precluding the misguided search for an "ontological foundation" for knowledge does *not* preclude ontological claims.

We may balk at the claim that knowledge, awareness, concepts, language, inference, justification, and the logical space of reasons all descend on the shoulders of the bright child somewhere around the age of four, without having existed in even the most primitive form hitherto. But we do not balk at the thought that a cluster of rights and responsibilities will descend on him on his eighteenth birthday, without having been present in even the most primitive form hitherto. The latter situation is, to be sure, more clear-cut than the former, since there is no mark of the former occasion save some adult's casual remark (e.g., "the kid knows what he's talking about"). But in both cases what has happened is a shift in a person's relations with others, not a shift inside the person which now *suits* him to enter such new relationships. (*PM*, 187)

Knowledge and truth claims are commodities traded in a community of human practices. They are the currency of distinctly *social* practices. Knowledge only happens in "the space of reasons," as Sellars puts it, which means that those social conditions determine and condition our knowledge. And not just in some "fallibilist" way, as a vague truism about cultural conditions influencing our ability to get correspondence right. No, what *counts* as "correspondence" is, at root, a *social* production. Social context is not a necessary evil that "taints" our ability to represent the world; rather, we are embedded in social practices that are the matrix from which all of our knowledge emerges. Epistemology will always be the ethnography of a particular people, what Hegel would call a particular but contingent *Sittlichkeit*. ("Only since Hegel," Rorty comments, "have philosophers begun toying with the notion that the individual apart from his society is just one more animal" [*PM*, 192].) But that also means that the practices *of* "justification" are going to be relative to that "society," that community *of* practice. To wish it otherwise is to wish away our finitude.

The Specter of Anti-Realism

Rorty, following Sellars and Quine, wants to disabuse us of thinking that language "represents" the world, "hooks onto" the world, or "corresponds to" the world. Our accounts of the world cannot be "analyzed" or reduced to something that is *extra*-linguistic—some "state of affairs" that is "just given" (what Sellars called the "Myth of the Given"). In short, there is no extra-linguistic "ground" or "foundation" for our knowing. Rather, truth, knowledge, and justification are features of *social* life and practices.

You can imagine the sort of response this will engender: What?! Are you saying there's nothing outside of language? Are you some kind of Berkleyan idealist? Do you think there's nothing outside of "texts"? Are you saying there's nothing "real"? Are you some kind of [gasp!] anti-realist?

Sigh.

The worry seems to be something like this: If Rorty (and Sellars and Kuhn and Wittgenstein) are right, then doesn't that mean our language doesn't "refer" to any*thing*? Aren't we then locked in some kind of idealism that doesn't "hook onto" or "refer" to the world? Are we locked inside our own minds, left to our own delusions?[12] If what is "real" or "true" is relative to a contingent "conceptual framework," then "something which seemed much like idealism began to become intellectually respectable" (275). (As becomes clear later, "idealism" and "anti-realism" are synonymous in this discussion [278].)

12. Here Rorty specifically focuses on issues in philosophy of science, mainly because that's where people think "reference" really matters and has traction (nobody's surprised, say, if it turns out that religion doesn't have a "real" referent [*PM*, 269]; on the other hand, it's precisely the desire to maintain this distinction that generates such angst from critics of Quine and Kuhn). In particular, this is framed as a matter of reference and translatability: "Did Newton give right answers to questions to which Aristotle had given wrong answers? Or were they asking different questions?" (266).

If the language is different, is the world different? If the terms change, do the things change? As we'll see, this becomes a question of whether there's "progress" in science (275), for if Aristotle and Newton weren't "really talking about" (268) the same thing, then it's harder to narrate a story of science's onward-and-upward progress from primitive hints to confident rationality.

However, Kuhn's work (and that of others) showed that, in fact, "the meaning of lots of statements in the language, including lots of 'observation' statements, got changed when a new theory came along" (270). In the face of these historical examples, the philosophers of reference (i.e., those defending "realism") conceded that observation was a kind of paradigm-relative interpretation; *however*, they began to argue, it must be the case that there are nonetheless extra-paradigm, "rational" criteria that can enable us to assess "rational" change (270–71). But this was only a "brief temptation" (271), because all the Quinean/Kuhnian reasons that precluded extra-paradigm criteria of observation also precluded extra-paradigm criteria for evaluating the shift from one paradigm to another (272). "The division of labor between the philosopher and the historian no longer made sense" (272).

Ultimately Rorty sees this as a "pseudo-issue" invented by Hilary Putnam and wryly comments: "It is difficult to find a philosopher who meets Putnam's criteria for being an 'antirealist'" (278; one might add it's equally difficult to find a living, breathing philosopher who fits the picture of Plantinga's "creative" antirealist).[13] Rorty tries to debunk a key misconception here: realist critics confuse having a theory of reference and granting a kind of ontological weight to things. That is, they think that having a theory of reference is the necessary condition for affirming that there are extra-paradigm "things." So they assume that if one rejects representation and correspondence, one is giving up on the metaphysical furniture of the universe. But those, like Dewey and James, who reject the "correspondence theory of truth," have "no sympathy" with an "inference from [A] 'one cannot give a theory-independent description of a thing' to the supposed conclusion that [B] 'there are no theory-independent things'" (279). So giving up on a theory of reference rooted in representationalism does *not* mean that the so-called anti-realist "will lack a story to tell about the causal effects upon our ancestors of the objects spoken of by the present theory" (282). Recognizing the social and communal conditions of knowledge—that our knowledge is *relative to* our social context—does not entail that everything is just "made up."

Consider an example from science, which is often taken to be the arbiter of "objective truth" par excellence. If past theories of, say, *phlogiston* didn't refer to some "thing" phlogiston, then doesn't it follow that no *present* theory refers to any such "thing" (*PM*, 285)? But Rorty again cautions about overstating the implications of his pragmatist (or holistic) account: "Now in one obvious sense we know perfectly well—prior to any theory—that they have been referring to the same things. They were all trying to *cope* with the same universe, and they referred to *it*"—and no revolution in paradigms would "put us out of touch with either the world or our ancestors" (286, emphasis added). Indeed, he's very explicit about this, citing Donald Davidson: "In giving up dependence on the concept of an uninterpreted reality, something outside all schemes and science, we do not relinquish the notion of objective truth—quite the contrary. . . . We do not give up the world,

13. In Alvin Plantinga, "The Twin Pillars of Christian Scholarship," in *Seeking Understanding: The Stob Lectures, 1986–1998* (Grand Rapids: Eerdmans, 2001), 128.

but reestablish unmediated touch with the familiar objects whose antics make our sentences and opinions true or false" (*PM*, 310).[14] Pragmatism rejects representation and correspondence; it doesn't reject the "antics" of things.

For Rorty, recognizing that justification is a social practice does not entail idealism or anti-realism. Idealism or anti-realism is just the flipside of the representationalist picture. It is precisely that picture that Rorty rejects—and the whole "package" that goes with it (inside/outside picture of mind and representation, a "naming" theory of the word-world relation, and a "correspondence" theory of truth). But Rorty can reject that "package" and yet *not* reject "reality" or "truth." He's just rejecting "objective" reality and "absolute" truth as rooted in representationalist realism. But he clearly affirms that we all inhabit a shared world that pushes back on us—the shared environment with which we "cope."[15] So perhaps we could think of Rorty affirming a realism without correspondence. And this, I will suggest, is just the sort of realism to which Christians should be committed—and that *for theological reasons* we should be suspicious of our default tendency to buy into representationalist realism. There might be good reasons for a Christian to be a "Rortyan."

Picturing "Pushback" in *Crazy Heart*

It's hard for us to shake our representationalist habits. This has become our default way of thinking about knowledge. The epistemological revolution commenced by Descartes has trickled down to the street and the pews so that we are all now comfortable thinking about knowledge as a relationship between an "inside" (mind) and an "outside" (world). Rorty presses us to recognize that the sort of thing knowledge is cannot be explained by mere passive response to an environment. Knowledge is a social, cultural *accomplishment*,

14. Citing Donald Davidson, "On the Very Idea of a Conceptual Scheme," *Proceedings and Addresses of the American Philosophical Association* 47 (1973–74): 5–20.

15. In *Philosophy and the Mirror of Nature*, this position is (at best) nascent and understated. But Rorty makes this more explicit in his "Response to Ramberg," in *Rorty and His Critics*, ed. Robert Brandom (Malden, MA: Blackwell, 2000), 370–76. My thanks to Ron Kuipers for helpful insights on this point.

which means that what *counts* as knowledge is inextricably linked to social life—to that infamous "circle of our peers."

As we've noted, this doesn't mean we are thereby free to just make stuff up—as if knowledge is therefore arbitrary and unconstrained. In rejecting "realist" representation, Rorty is not advocating for "anti-realism" or "idealism" since that would just be the inversion of representationalism. To the contrary, Rorty's account of *social* justification actually doubles up the constraints: on the one hand, we still have to grapple with the "antics" of things; on the other hand, we are simultaneously accountable to a *community* of fellow knowers. Sure, Rorty makes the unnerving claim that truth is what your peers will let you get away with saying. But here's the thing: your peers aren't going to let you get away with saying just anything! To emphasize that epistemic justification is rooted in a community of social practice is not tantamount to denying that knowledge can be justified; it is to shift the locus of justification. And that means that our claims to knowledge can also be *un*justified if our "peers" won't let us get away with it. Too many philosophers hear Rorty's account of social justification *as if* it denied justification or unhooked knowledge claims from any standard of accountability, leaving us to whim, fantasy, and power plays. But that's not Rorty's point at all; to the contrary, I think it is the representationalist account that abandons knowledge to the "private" relationship of individuals to some "exterior" reality. In contrast, Rorty's account resituates all knowers within a community of epistemic accountability, without recourse to magical appeals to "the way things are." All sorts of deluded people are "realists."

These dynamics are illustrated in Scott Cooper's Oscar-winning film *Crazy Heart* (2009), starring Jeff Bridges as "Bad" Blake and Maggie Gyllenhaal as Jean, a journalist who draws him out of his delusions.

We first meet Bad climbing out of his dilapidated pickup truck after a long drive to a gig at a bowling alley in Nowheresville, Arizona. This is a long way from the life he enjoyed as a headliner in the realms of country music stardom. In a film where song lyrics drive the narrative and provide important psychological clues, it's no accident that the first number we hear Bad perform is one of his best-known hits, "Somebody Else," in which he laments,

> I used to be somebody
> but now I am somebody else.

> Who I'll be tomorrow
> is anybody's guess.

After which he proceeds to exit stage left and vomit in the nearest trash can.

The Bad Blake we meet is already somebody else. His alcoholism has derailed his creativity and squandered his gifts and resources. He is a sad shell of a man, and when, in that opening scene, he emerges from the truck and pours a bottle of his urine on the ground, you don't know whether to be disgusted by him or feel sorry for him. Chased by aging women who are just as sad and lonely, Bad is on a downward spiral of self-destruction, not least because he lives in his own reality. The alcohol is like a private epistemic framework—an idiosyncratic prism that refracts a distorted world in which he lives. It is an isolating, desocializing habit that leaves him ensconced in his own delusions—that he's fine, that the problem is other people. The biggest delusion—and the one that is most often challenged—is that his ways have no repercussions for others. This is captured in his biggest hit, "Fallin' and Flyin'," in which he confesses,

> I was goin' where I shouldn't go,
> Seein' who I shouldn't see,
> Doin' what I shouldn't do,
> Bein' who I shouldn't be.
>
> A little voice told me it's all wrong,
> Another voice told me it's all right.
> I used to think that I was strong,
> But lately I've just lost the fight.
>
> *It's funny how fallin' feels like flyin'*
> *for a little while.*
> *Funny how fallin' feels like flyin'*
> *for a little while.*

But then the song takes an unapologetic, unrepentant turn.

> I got tired of being good,
> Started missin' that ol' feelin' free
> Stopped actin' like I thought I should
> And went on back to bein' me.

> I never meant to hurt no one.
> I just had to have my way
> If there's such a thing as too much fun,
> This must be the price you pay.

So the epistemic ambiguity in the song takes on a new significance that we could formulate in Rortyan terms: If you think you're flyin', but all your peers are telling you you're fallin', there might be good reason to think your "knowledge" is not justified, even if you think it "represents" reality.

One can "read" the movie with this Rortyan concern in mind, in which case we'll notice two intertwining threads in the story. On the one hand, the "antics of things" push and pull Bad in ways that challenge his take on the world. While the alcohol encourages him to be either a deluded realist or a hoodwinked idealist, the world is going to persistently push back on him. On the other hand, it is precisely *others*—his "peers"—who are going to play a crucial role in reshaping his engagement with the world. You might say that neither the world nor his friends are going to let him "get away with" his alcoholic construal of things.

We see a string of friends and relationships who refuse to enable his whiskey-fueled misperceptions. His longtime friend, Wayne, is a bartender (of all things!) who refuses to enable him, constantly pressing him to get help. Even his rather slimy agent paternalistically tries to manage Bad's finances so that he doesn't drink himself into destitution. But that circle of peers gets a special jolt when he meets the music journalist, Jean, and her son, Buddy. Bad's growing affection and love for them calls him out of his isolation and epistemic insularity. He is pulled out of the distorted privacy of his alcoholic perception and *called* to be someone else by his love for "Jeannie" and her son. They become a whole new world for him. His selfishness dissolves in their presence, and he becomes a servant of interests beyond himself. He even begins to realize that he *has* hurt others, including a son he abandoned when the child was only four years old. Jeannie is waking him up to himself.

He inhabits the world anew, and is willing to answer this "call" from the world of Jean and Buddy in radical ways. So when Jean asks him not to drink in front of Buddy, he answers, "No problem."

Except that it is. Addictions die hard. The first time Jean leaves Buddy in Bad's care, he keeps his promise. But a day without

drinking nearly kills him. The world—even the world of his making—pushes back in disruptive ways. When he reaches out to his
own son, with hopes of starting a relationship, the son refuses.
The world won't bend to his will. When he continues drinking and
crashes his truck in a drunken stupor, his near death is another sign
that the world is not going to let him "get away with" the construal
he's lived with up until this point. And neither are his peers.

This culminates in a frightening episode: when Bad watches
Buddy in the mall for a while, he stops by a bar for "just one drink."
But in the blink of an eye, Buddy is gone. Police are searching for
him, and Jean arrives at the security office both distraught and
angry, and refuses to let Bad comfort her. When Buddy is (thank-
fully!) found safe, Bad cozies up to Jean and mumbles apologeti-
cally: "You know I wouldn't do anything to hurt the boy."

"But you *did*," Jean retorts. She gathers Buddy in a flurry and
heads home, breaking all contact with Bad. He's now lost the
love that had called him out of himself, and so he spirals back
into that drunk, deluded self in a final binge that takes him to the
very bottom. Humiliated, half awake, but broken and disgusted
with himself, he finally calls his friend: "Wayne," he says. "I want
to get sober."

A Rortyan analysis will note two things about this turn in the
story. First, what Rorty called "the antics" of things have a kind of
ontological weight about them that won't let us say just whatever
we *want* about them. There are ways in which the world won't let
you get away with unsustainable construals. Bad construals (i.e.,
Bad's construals) are simply not able to *cope* with the obduracy
of things: his body can't do what he thinks it can; and Jean won't
tolerate his take on things. In other words, she won't let him "get
away with" it any longer.

Second, Bad's turning point is a result of being enfolded into a
new community of "peers"—the rehab community he enters with
Wayne's help. That *social* context is not just a biological detox; it
is also a social reconfiguration of his epistemic frameworks. The
truth is not something Bad can "access" on his own. Because truth
is a *social* reality, Bad needs a community in order to see the truth
about himself. He enters a new "space of reasons," you might
say, when he confesses to the group: "Couple of days ago, I lost a
little boy. I was drunk. Been drunk most of my life. Lost a helluva
lot." To emphasize the dependence of our knowledge on social

conditions is not a retreat from reality into some fantasy land where we can just make stuff up. It's not that knowledge is *either* social *or* "objective"; rather, objectivity is a social accomplishment. Losing our illusions of independence might just be a way for us to be found, and to find truth in the right community of practice.

Rethinking "Objectivity"

In a way that is slightly idiosyncratic, Rorty extols "hermeneutics" as what we do when we get over the ingrained compulsion to "do" epistemology. But, he emphasizes, hermeneutics is not the "successor" to epistemology (*PM*, 315); it's not the new way of "doing" epistemology. Hermeneutics is the *refusal* of epistemology, resisting the temptation to "ground" knowledge or truth or justification in something extra-social or extra-linguistic. Or, to put this otherwise, hermeneutics gives up on the assumption that ultimately all discourses are "commensurable"—that all of our differences can be resolved by finding some game-transcendent "common ground" or extra-social "foundation" or game-above-all-games "neutral language" that would reduce all differences to agreement. "The assumption that an epistemology can be constructed is the assumption that such common ground exists" (316). That there is such a game-independent foundation, of course, is just what Rorty (like Wittgenstein) rejects.[16]

16. However, Rorty is willing to make an interesting concession: we might save the term "epistemology" for an ethnography of epistemic practices where there is widespread consensus. Here he draws on Kuhn's distinction between "normal" science and "abnormal" science (or "revolutionary" science). As Kuhn puts it, when a regnant paradigm is in place—that is, when there is widespread consensus about the paradigm—it governs the practices, institutions, and criteria of science. In short, the paradigm specifies what constitutes scientific "orthodoxy," and those carrying out research within its parameters conduct "normal" science. Those who bristle against the paradigm are, in a sense, scientific heretics. They might be scientific revolutionaries in the making (Galileo), and they might just be "kooks" (e.g., Gall's phrenology).

In this respect, "normal science is as close as real life comes to the epistemologist's notion of what it is to be rational. Everybody agrees on how to evaluate everything everybody else says" (*PM*, 320). So one can get pretty confident about achieving "epistemological commensuration" when "we already have agreed-upon practices of inquiry" (321). The problem is that such widespread consensus tends to cover over the fact that this is a paradigm, that this is the product of social consensus, and thus fails to appreciate the contingency of "normal science." Instead, what's been agreed

However, because we've bought into an account that identifies "rationality" with just such a dreamed-of common ground/foundation, the rejection of this seems like a license for *ir*-rationality. The pragmatist's abandonment of the quest for "commensuration" is decried as "relativism" (by which is usually meant sheer arbitrariness). And giving up on commensuration (i.e., agreement based on *one* foundation or a universal language) seems to give up on agreement altogether. Rorty is not unfamiliar with these worries: "Holistic theories," he recognizes, "seem to license everyone to construct his own little whole—his own little paradigm, his own little practice, his own little language-game—and then crawl into it" (*PM*, 317).

In response to these sorts of worries, Rorty seems to offer two replies: (1) foundationalism is not the only way to be "rational"; and (2) commensuration is not the only way to seek agreement or consensus. So the holist/pragmatist does not give up on rationality; he or she just thinks the (performative) criteria for what counts as "rational" are not what our referentialist theories would suggest. Nor does the holist/pragmatist retreat into enclaves or proverbial "choirs"; rather, she pursues agreement *in conversation*, as an effect of persuasion. "The hope for agreement is never lost so long as the conversation lasts" (318). The conversation in a social community is the locus of our "justification," but that conversation is had by "peers" who inhabit a shared formation, who together feel the pushback of the world with which we all cope. So to say that justification is a matter of convention is not to take us out of the "real" world but rather to locate us solidly within it, with all of its contingency and particularity. The community of practice that is the locus of meaning is always already embedded in the world.

This means we need to rethink (and redeem) the notion of "objectivity." Critics "have helped perpetuate the dogma that only where there is correspondence to reality is there the possibility of rational agreement" understood as "objective" truth (333). In many ways, Rorty's therapy is concerned with healing us of such binary, all-or-nothing framings of the matter—freeing us up to imagine

---

upon is just identified with rationality per se. What's conventional is taken as if it were "natural." But Rorty's holism would point out that the best we can say is that this is the fruit of a long and successful conversation. In this respect, "epistemology" should own up to being the ethnography of a long and successful game that is nonetheless contingent and conventional, resting on a whole set of social practices and habits.

other ways of being "rational"—or, perhaps better, freeing us up to see that effectively and *in practice* we already work with other functional modes of rationality, and that "objective" is just an honorific name we give to those positions that enjoy widespread consensus. "The applications of such honorifics as 'objective' and 'cognitive' is never anything more than an expression of the presence of, or the hope for, agreement among inquirers" (335).[17] In that respect "our only *usable* notion of 'objectivity' is 'agreement' rather than mirroring" (337, emphasis added). As he nicely puts it, in a way that honors creational finitude, "We should not regret our inability to perform a feat which no one has any idea how to perform" (340).

What we spend most of our time doing, Rorty might say, is not "knowing," but *coping*. Indeed, "the word *knowledge* would not seem worth fighting over were it not for the Kantian tradition

17. Rorty spends the next few pages contesting the false binary of "realism" and "idealism," taking up criticisms of Thomas Kuhn's account of scientific rationality as rooted in practice (in his landmark work *The Structure of Scientific Revolutions*, which Rorty celebrates as a "hermeneutic" account of natural science). Kuhn's critics worry that, by rejecting a pristine "realism" and by recognizing the role of social practices in determining scientific knowledge, Kuhn reduces science to something we "make up" about the world—which seems obviously ludicrous. "Here we come round once again to the bugbear of 'idealism' [or "anti-realism"] and the notion that the search for an algorithm goes hand in hand with a 'realistic' approach to science whereas a relaxation into the merely hermeneutic method of the historian sells the pass to the idealist" (*PM*, 342). This is because, to the realist, anything that is not realism is idealism or anti-realism. So when Kuhn points out the extent to which scientific knowledge is rooted in communities of practice, "an attempt to make the world 'malleable to the human will' is suspected. This produces, yet again, the positivist claim that we must either make a clear distinction between the 'noncognitive' and the 'cognitive,' or else 'reduce' the former to the latter. For the third possibility—reducing the latter to the former [which critics think Kuhn is doing]—seems to 'spiritualize' nature by making it like history or literature, something which men have *made* rather than something they *find*" (342).

But for Rorty, this is a muddled critique based on faulty assumptions: "The muddle consists in suggesting that Kuhn, by 'reducing' the methods of scientists to those of politicians, has 'reduced' the 'found' world of neutrons to the 'made' world of social relationships." But in so doing, the "realist" reduces knowledge to the sort of thing that could be acquired by machines (this will be an important point for Robert Brandom): "Here again we find the notion that whatever cannot be discovered by a machine programmed with the appropriate algorithm cannot exist 'objectively,' and thus must be somehow a 'human creation.'" But "the distinction between epistemology and hermeneutics should not be thought of as paralleling a distinction between what is 'out there' and what we 'make up'" (342).

that to be a philosopher is to have a 'theory of knowledge,' and the Platonic tradition that action not based on knowledge of the truth of propositions is 'irrational'" (356). But pragmatism contests both of those requirements, not in order to celebrate irrationality, but rather to call into question our reductionistic picture of "true" knowledge as correspondence—a picture that fails to appreciate our contingency and social dependence *as* knowers. We might simply say that Rorty's "hermeneutics" extols the priority of know-*how*, whereas we have largely fallen into the habit of reducing knowledge to know-*that*. And know-*how* is not *un*-true: it is true differently.

Certainly questions remain. There is a kind of queasiness that often accompanies an appreciation of Rorty's argument. We remain haunted by questions that seem unanswered. Rorty's reply is to usually quip, "Well, stop asking those questions! Why do you persist in talking that way?"[18] The questions and uneasiness are themselves effects of a misbegotten paradigm, he would say. But let's ask them nonetheless and see if we can divine a Rortyan reply.

Does Rorty Deny "Objectivity"?

No and yes. *If* by "objectivity" you mean a final language that transcends the contingency of practice—some sort of pristine way to get a one-on-one correspondence to "the way things are" ("the final commensurating vocabulary for all *possible* rational discourse" [*PM*, 387])—then *yes*, Rorty denies "objectivity."

18. The point is that some "problems" are pseudoproblems and the very attempt to answer them lends credence to the fiction created by epistemology. In a later work, Rorty retorts,

> There is a difference between hoping for the end of Philosophy 101 and hoping for the end of philosophy. I am still thought of (as by Putnam . . .) as recommending "the end of philosophy," despite my explicit rejection of this label on the last page of *Philosophy and the Mirror of Nature* and my attempts in subsequent writings to scrape it off. Perhaps it may clarify matters if I say that I hope that people will never stop reading, e.g., Plato, Aristotle, Kant, and Hegel, but also hope that they will, sooner or later, stop trying to sucker freshmen into taking an interest in the Problem of the External World and the Problem of Other Minds.

See Rorty, "Hilary Putnam and the Relativist Menace," in *Truth and Progress: Philosophical Papers* (Cambridge: Cambridge University Press, 1998), 3:47n16. I'm grateful to Ron Kuipers for helping me track down this reference.

But *if* you mean something like "truth," then *no*, Rorty doesn't deny this; he just situates it. Seeking "truth" in this respect is "just one among many ways in which we might be edified" (360). He doesn't deny that "objectivity" is a game you can play. It's "perfectly possible and frequently actual," but it should not be "transcendentalized" as either the game-above-all-games or the "foundation" of every other game. It's a game you can play. And we shouldn't paper over the *contingency* of "objectivity"[19]—it's just a shorthand term for "conformity to the norms of justification . . . we find about us" (361; cf. 335). "Objectively true" is our quickest and cleanest way to communicate that a claim is something we can easily make in our current "paradigm," just as "corresponds to how things are" is "an automatic compliment paid to successful normal discourse" (372). Or, "'objective truth' is no more and no less than the best idea we currently have about how to explain what is going on" (385). What we *agree* is "objectively" true are those claims that enable us to *cope* with the world.

That's also why *if* by "objective" you mean something like "there's a world that 'shoves back' at us," then *no*, Rorty does *not* deny this. He just thinks we should stop confusing this—what he calls "things' obduracy"—with some magical claim to have "represented" reality (375).[20] So Rorty certainly does *not* deny that "we are shoved around by physical reality" (375). The question is, "What does being shoved around have to do with objectivity, accurate representation, or correspondence?" We don't "make contact" with reality (that assumes the inside/outside picture that negates the contingency of our social environment); rather, we *deal with* reality. We make our way in the world by means of a know-*how* for which we are indebted to—and dependent upon—a community of meaning making. It is our social dependency *as* "knowers" (know-*how*-ers) that Rorty thinks is ignored by representationalist

---

19. Such a project exhibits "the urge to see social practices of justification as more than just such practices" (*PM*, 390)—which often ends up *naturalizing* knowledge, treating us like photocells or thermostats, rather than seeing knowledge (and hence "truth") as a social accomplishment. We will return to these themes with Robert Brandom in the next chapter.

20. "The absence of description is confused with a privilege attaching to a certain description. Only by such a confusion can the inability to offer individuating conditions for the one true description of material things be confused with insensitivity to the things' obduracy" (*PM*, 375).

accounts. So rather than seeing Rorty as a pesky gadfly who simply takes sophomoric delight in deflating the pretensions of "realist" accounts, we should see his constructive, positive project as a renewed appreciation for the contingent, social conditions of our knowledge. And as I have tried to suggest, I think that intersects with a Christian philosophical account that takes seriously the conditions of creaturehood.

Is Rorty a "Relativist"?

Yes and no. *If* by relativist you really mean a "nihilist" or an indifferent, amoral aesthete who thinks "anything goes," then *no*, Rorty is not a relativist since he clearly makes *valuations* between societies and extols liberal democracy (even "America") as *better* than other social configurations. This is not some hypocritical contradiction in his thought; instead, it is an indicator that any reading that reduces Rorty to nihilistic "anything-goes" indifference has failed to appreciate the nuances of his account. There is more than one way to *not* be a nihilist.[21] So, no, Rorty is not that sort of "relativist."

But *if* by "relativist" you mean that he sees such valuations as *relative to* and *dependent upon* contingent social practices and communities of discourse, then *yes* Rorty is a relativist (*PM*, 377). *But who isn't?* is Rorty's reply (374, 385). This point is crucial, especially for Christians seeking to critically appropriate Rorty's pragmatism as a philosophy of creaturehood. In fact, Rorty frames this in stark terms that cast a kind of theological shadow on the issues: "The notion of an unclouded Mirror of Nature is the notion of a mirror which would be indistinguishable from what was mirrored, and thus would not be a mirror at all. The notion of a human being whose mind is such an unclouded mirror, and who *knows* this, is the image, as Sartre says, of God" (376). Now many representationalists are going to invoke all sorts of "fallibilist" qualifications here, emphasizing that while they claim "objective" knowledge,

---

21. "Just as the moral philosopher who sees virtue as Aristotelian self-development is thought to lack concern for his fellow man, so the epistemologist who is merely behaviorist is treated as one who does not share the universal human aspiration toward objective truth" (*PM*, 376). But the latter criticism of behaviorist "epistemology" is just as wrong as that criticism of Aristotelian eudaemonism.

they don't pretend to "pristine" knowledge, and so on. But Rorty's point is not deflected by fallibilist qualifications, because he is arguing that the very picture of the "objective" knower denies aspects of our creaturehood—namely, our contingency, dependency, and sociality. Even the fallibilist "objective" knower (i.e., representer) is purportedly able to do this *on her own*. The picture is fundamentally individualist and atomistic: the lone knower, however "limited," confronted by—and mirroring, however opaquely—the "external" world. Even the fallibilist representationalist "knower" is godlike insofar as she *doesn't seem to depend on anyone*.[22]

Now, a Christian "realist" might say that she is ultimately dependent on *God*, but I think Rorty's account is actually more attuned to the fact that, as creatures dependent upon God, we have been made to be dependent on others. Our dependence on the divine is inextricably bound up with our dependence on other human beings. This is why we are not merely dependent but also *social*. We are social *because* we are dependent. Rorty's pragmatism—his "relativism"—is a philosophical account that recognizes and embraces the depth of our contingency and dependence. Pragmatism ends up being an unintended philosophy of the Creator/creature distinction.

This is also why Rorty sees something *in*human about the realist/representationalist picture. It functionally ascribes to us a kind of godlike independence; at the same time, it seems to efface our humanity—it leads to "the dehumanization of human beings."

> To abandon the notion that philosophy must show all possible discourse naturally converging to a consensus [the assumption of "realism" and its notion of "objectivity"] . . . would be to abandon the hope of being anything more than merely human. It would thus be to abandon the Platonic notions of Truth and Reality and Goodness as entities which may not be even dimly mirrored by present practices and beliefs, and to settle back into the "relativism" which assumes that our only useful notions of "true" and "real" and "good" are extrapolations from those practices and beliefs. (PM, 377)[23]

22. This is precisely why I think the language of "absolute" truth that *creatures* would "have" is a signal of a certain arrogation of our epistemic capacities to godlike status.

23. Given the historic Christian affirmation of the Transcendentals (Goodness, Truth, Beauty), below I will grapple with the implications of absorbing Rorty's point here vis-à-vis the tradition of "Christian Platonism."

Is Rorty a "relativist"? Yes, in just this sense: that our knowledge is rooted in, and dependent upon, contingent social practices reflective of the communities of which we are a part. This only feels "deflationary" because a certain philosophical tradition has *in*flated our capacities and expectations in this regard. By recognizing, affirming, and analyzing the dynamics of our finite, social dependence, you might say Rorty is the "realist": his philosophy does not expect divine abilities from human knowers; his account of knowledge is cut to the measure of finite, contingent creatures.

And once again, Rorty replies to the smug dismissal of the realist with a challenge: "Who *isn't* a relativist?" Show me an account of knowledge that isn't relativist, Rorty says, and I'll show you one that forgets where it came from, one that denies our finitude, dependence, contingency, and sociality. Show me an account that promises to deliver "the way things are," and I'll show you an account that has forgotten and papered over the communal, social matrix from which that account was born—one that has failed to appreciate the *contingency* of its vocabulary.

This does *not* entail skepticism. To recognize contingency is *not* the equivalent of saying "anything goes." To appreciate the contingency of our "take" on the world—and it is always *our* take, a socially shared take—is not a covert way of saying that all takes are *arbitrary*. There are good and bad construals, better and worse accounts. But "good" and "better" accounts are not so because they have managed to mirror reality and escape the contingent, social conditions of knowing. No, good and better accounts are those that better enable us to *cope* with the obduracy of things, the "antics" of things, as collectively discerned by our peers.[24] We can recognize the contingency of *our* "take" on the world and still affirm it as the *best* account of the world (indeed, of the entire cosmos, including the divine).[25] We just don't get to "secure" this by

24. Rorty's "coping" shouldn't be heard as a mere survivalism, as if to "cope" with the world is to just "get by." Instead Rorty means to capture a fundamentally *practical* picture of our being-in-the-world: to "cope" with the world is to make our way in the world as practical (pragmatic) actors and doers, not merely to perceive the world as observers or spectators.

25. There is no inherent reason why pragmatism needs to be a naturalism. Rorty will sometimes seem to suggest otherwise since he takes pragmatism to be an unremitting embrace of contingency and finitude. But as I hope we've seen, the biblical doctrine of creation yields the same recognition (and affirmation) of finitude and contingency

representational magic that effectively overcomes the contingency and dependence. This obviously has implications for Christian confession and witness: it would mean that a Christian "take" on the world is contingent. But as I hope to show, recognizing its contingency does not undercut its claim to *truth*.

"Realism" without Correspondence

Let's grant that there are clearly legitimate worries in the ballpark of a "Christian pragmatism." It still *feels* like Wittgenstein and Rorty's rejection of representation, and hence realism, must deny "reality." We're probably still left with this feeling in the pit of our stomachs, a visceral, nagging worry that the transcendent God will be eviscerated by such social accounts of knowledge. If all of our knowledge is contingent, social, dependent, and relative, then isn't *God* contingent, a product of *our* creative impulses? If the "justification" of our knowledge is tethered to social practices, then shouldn't we be worried that our peers won't let us get away with confessing that "Jesus is Lord?" Or worse: we might be haunted by the fact that our "peers" *do* let us "get away with it," but that it's not really *true*. Doesn't Christian faith *require* that our claims about God "correspond" to the reality of God? Isn't it important that we secure the representational capacity of our language in order to ensure all of our God-talk is not a fiction?[26] Maybe we're willing to entertain pragmatism for "this-worldly" claims, but the stakes seem to be raised if we are talking about Christian confessional claims about the transcendent God.

Given contemporary discussions in theology, especially in the orbit of postliberal theology and Radical Orthodoxy, the technical

---

without the overreaching claim that "the natural" is all there is. Naturalism might often attend pragmatism, but it is not entailed by pragmatism.

26. This is the core question of Kevin Hector's *Theology without Metaphysics: God, Language, and the Spirit of Recognition* (Cambridge: Cambridge University Press, 2011), a book that came into my hands late in the process of finishing this book. It was also a core question of my earlier book *Speech and Theology*. The difference between the present book and Hector's is that I am not only or narrowly considering the conditions of God-talk. I think the conditions for God-talk are the same conditions for all "talk." (I would note that D. Stephen Long addresses the same problem under the rubric of worries about "fideism" in *Speaking of God: Theology, Language, and Truth* [Grand Rapids: Eerdmans, 2009]).

philosophical and theological question here can be formulated in a couple of different ways. Both of these are concerned with the same problem, but they raise the issue slightly differently. For example, we could ask, Can there be a Christian theology without realism, without "metaphysics"? This is how D. Stephen Long tackles the challenge of pragmatism in his important book *Speaking of God: Theology, Language, and Truth*: "Many find in Wittgenstein's philosophy a critique of metaphysics, even another pronouncement of its end. If so, it would hold forth little promise in bringing together theology and a metaphysical philosophy" (like that of Thomas Aquinas).[27] If metaphysics *is* realism, and Christian theology assumes such a realist metaphysics, then it would seem that the pragmatist rejection of realism would entail a rejection of Christian theology.

On the other hand, yet very much akin to the first question, we might put the question this way: How could we have a *participatory* ontology—a strong claim that all of creation is "suspended" in the gracious creative power of the Creator—and yet extol *nominalism*, a metaphysical view that rejects the notion of Platonic universals and Forms?

I should explain the back story to this second version of the question. In the history of philosophy, a broadly "Platonic" doctrine of "universals" asserts that what makes *this* tree a tree is that this particular, individuated tree "participates" in the Form of *treeness*; and what makes *this* sculpture beautiful is that it participates in the Form of Beauty. These Forms are "universals" in the sense that they are the one standard for the *essence* of things; indeed, things only "are" to the extent that they participate in these Forms. And the Forms/universals are what's *really real*. So Platonic universalism is an ultimate *realism*.[28] Given deep resonances between this metaphysical picture and Christian theological convictions, this account

27. Long, *Speaking of God*, 215. Long is actually taking up the counterintuitive task of showing that "Wittgenstein proves helpful for the recovery of metaphysics and its reconciliation with theology" (ibid.). As he later puts it, Wittgenstein "critiques a 'meta' that is 'beyond' without being 'in the midst of'" (221).

28. Though there are legitimate questions about whether the Platonic picture was also "representationalist." Both Rorty and folks like Milbank and Pickstock would say not, and that we shouldn't anachronistically read our modernist representationalism back into the ancients. See Rorty, *PM*, 46–48; and Milbank and Pickstock, *Truth in Aquinas*, 1–6.

became de facto orthodoxy for the Christian tradition, adopted by Augustine, Aquinas, and others.[29] The result was a "sacramental" understanding of creation "charged" with the glory of God, as Gerard Manley Hopkins once put it. In other words, a *creational* ontology is a *participatory* ontology that emphasizes that creation *is* just to the extent that it participates in (or is "suspended from") the Creator.[30] So it would seem that a robust Christian metaphysics is inextricably linked with Platonic *realism*.

However, in the later Middle Ages, certain shifts took place in metaphysics around just this matter of "universals" and realism. Late medieval thinkers like William of Ockham and Duns Scotus came to suspect that metaphysical entities like "Forms" of tree-ness were awfully superfluous. So they effectively rejected such "universals" and instead asserted that *we* merely "name" things in ways that categorize them in this way. In other words, what makes a tree a "tree" is not its participation in some fictive Form of *treeness* but rather *our* bottom-up practice of *naming* various things "trees." Hence their view, in contrast with a doctrine of (Platonic) universals, is often described as *nominalism*, from the Latin word for "name," *nom*.[31]

There is an added layer at stake here: scholars such as Charles Taylor, John Milbank, Brad Gregory, and Hans Boersma have also told a story about modernity in which this metaphysical shift away

29. For a succinct summary of how and why this was the case, see Hans Boersma's discussion of Platonic realism in *Heavenly Participation: The Weaving of a Sacramental Tapestry* (Grand Rapids: Eerdmans, 2010), 79–80.

30. See my extended discussion of "participation" in *Introducing Radical Orthodoxy: Mapping a Post-Secular Theology* (Grand Rapids: Baker Academic, 2005), 87–122. I would note that, while I think a creational ontology will be fundamentally a "participatory" ontology insofar as it describes the relationship between the Creator and creation, I'm less convinced that this requires a Christian metaphysic to *also* subscribe to a specifically Platonic account of the Forms to account for things like the "essence" of "treeness." It seems to me that a broadly participatory account of the Creator/creation relation is separable from the specifics of a Platonic theory of the Forms.

31. Again, for a fuller but still succinct discussion of these matters, see Boersma, *Heavenly Participation*, 79–81; and Smith, *Introducing Radical Orthodoxy*, 95–103. It might be important to point out, of course, that nominalism was *not* an idealism; the nominalists did not deny a "real world." In other words, while we set up a supposed dichotomy between "realism" and "nominalism," we shouldn't too hastily conclude that nominalism denied "reality," even *divine* reality. (Scotus, a Franciscan, wasn't denying the existence of God.)

from participation to mere nominalism effectively "severed" creation from the Creator, unhooking the world from its participation in God, and thus cutting creation loose to become the flattened, enclosed, "secular" world we now inhabit. On this account, nominalism is what leads us to "a secular age" and the unraveling of the "sacramental tapestry."[32]

That is the historical and theological background, then, to a pointed question: Given that Rorty's pragmatism is often described as a form of *nominalism*,[33] how could Christian theology possibly be reconciled with—let alone aided by—pragmatism? It would seem that *transcendence* is at stake. Or, to put it otherwise, it would seem that a "sacramental" understanding of creation demands a realism that, in turn, requires us to reject the "nominalism" of pragmatism. If that's the case, then you can *either* have a sacramental ontology *or* be a pragmatist.

As you might guess, the (Christian) pragmatist response is to refuse this as a false dichotomy. Now there will certainly be pragmatists (indeed, most) who reject the entire picture of a "sacramental" ontology along with the notion that the cosmos *is* insofar as it participates in the transcendent God. And there will be pragmatists who assert that their denial is entailed by their pragmatism. But that is overreaching on their part. While pragmatists (especially in the vein of William James and John Dewey) tend to be predisposed toward metaphysical minimalism and naturalism, that's more like a personality trait than a logical entailment of a pragmatist account of meaning.[34] While pragmatism tends to be skeptical about a pro-

32. For the fullest statement, see Brad Gregory, *The Unintended Reformation: How a Religious Revolution Secularized Society* (Cambridge, MA: Harvard University Press, 2012). It should be noted that this story is contested. See, most recently, Richard Muller, "Not Scotist: Understandings of Being, Univocity, and Analogy in Early Modern Reformed Thought," *Reformation and Renaissance Review* 14 (2012): 125–48.

33. Though Rorty's embrace of the term would have to be qualified: this would seem to be akin to describing himself as an "anti-realist"—which he does *not* do precisely because the options "realist" *or* "anti-realist" are generated by the same problematic assumption regarding representation. Similarly, it seems to me that Rorty would reject "Platonic" universals without necessarily being entirely comfortable with being described as a "nominalist."

34. As Jeffrey Stout remarks, "Pragmatism, understood strictly as a critique of metaphysics in the pejorative sense, need not be troubled by any of this, taken simply as a story faithfully believed. Its quarrel is not with the God of Amos and Dorothy Day, or even with the God of Barthian theology, but with the God of Descartes, and

liferation of metaphysical entities beyond the natural, it is not a metaphysical police force that simply rules out the transcendent. As an account of meaning, pragmatism is not some philosophical clerk that claims to have exhaustively enumerated all of the ontological furniture of the cosmos and is thereby able to say "X does not exist." In short, pragmatism does not preclude the existence of God; and therefore it doesn't rule out a "sacramental" cosmos per se.

Then what is the tension? Let's remember what "pragmatism" involves, at least as we've been engaging it in this book. Following Wittgenstein, pragmatism argues that meaning is primarily *use* rather than reference. We make our way in the world on the basis of a know-*how* that is acquired through practice, absorbed from our immersion in a community of practice that "trains" us how to grapple with the world rather than "mirroring" reality. Knowledge is more like "coping" with the world, as Rorty puts it. Thus pragmatists reject *referentialist* or *representationalist* accounts of meaning and knowledge that posit a kind of magical hook between ideas "inside" my mind and things "outside" my mind. Instead, referential claims are understood as games we've learned to play *from* a community of practice.

This is why, at its heart, pragmatism should be understood as a philosophy of contingency, dependence, and community. Meaning and knowledge are social accomplishments that *depend* on our relationships to communities of practice and an environment with which we grapple. It is in this sense that pragmatism is a *relativism* in a technical sense: it emphasizes that, because we are finite, contingent, historical, social creatures, our knowledge is *relative to* the communities of practice that "gift" us with the ability to cope with the world. Hence pragmatism rejects the representationalist picture as atomistic, individualist hubris: as if we could "know" *on our own*. Representationalism denies our dependence, positing an independent knower whose interior representations "mirror" reality.

There is a tension between pragmatism and a "sacramental" ontology—between "nominalism" and a Christian-Platonic "realism"—*only* insofar as this sacramental "realism" binds itself

<hr />

with the God of analytic metaphysics. Its account of excellence, like its account of obligation, can accommodate whatever persons, social relationships, and practices there happen to be. Its purpose should not be to put theologically inclined citizens on the defensive." *Democracy and Tradition* (Princeton, NJ: Princeton University Press, 2004), 268.

to *representationalism*. But it need not (and should not) do so. Keep in mind, pragmatism does not preclude referential claims; it just precludes the representationalist picture that allegedly "grounds" such claims. Instead, Wittgenstein and Rorty emphasize that our referential claims are successful "moves" in a game we've learned to play with others who share our world. Our referential claims are "true" insofar as our peers let us get away with them—and if they are *good* claims that help us "cope" with the world, then the community of our linguistic peers *will* let us "get away with" them. Pragmatism doesn't insulate us from the world, from "reality"; it just denies the picture of the knower as a lone representer whose mind (independently) mirrors reality.

A sacramental ontology, with its Christian "realism," aims to affirm and guard two things: (1) the reality and *in*dependence of the transcendent God on whom creation depends for its existence; and (2) the participatory relation of created reality "in" God (per Acts 17; Col. 2).[35] The question is, Are either of these features of a sacramental ontology somehow precluded by pragmatism? Or, in other words, do either of these features of a sacramental ontology require *representationalism*? If not, then we need not choose *between* either pragmatism *or* a sacramental ontology.

Addressing a similar set of questions and concerns, Stephen Long argues that Wittgenstein's pragmatism is not essentially hostile to something like a Thomistic metaphysics (a prime example of what I've been calling a "sacramental ontology"). "Would Wittgenstein deny truth to theology?," he asks.

> Despite his many protestations against the use of metaphysics, if metaphysics is understood as the adequacy of language to accomplish something more than its own context would permit, then Wittgenstein's work is no part of the "end of metaphysics," but its retrieval. His realism makes metaphysics necessary even when he worries that realism is just the flipside of idealism seeking to match language in our head to things in the world. Wittgenstein teaches us not to confuse representation with realism.[36]

Thus Long proposes a realism without representation.

---

35. So creation is "nothing" *in itself*. For a provocative exposition of this theme, see Conor Cunningham, *Genealogy of Nihilism* (London: Routledge, 2002).
36. Long, *Speaking of God*, 300.

But he still retains a commitment to "correspondence"; that is, Long assumes that any Christian metaphysic that is going to retain aspects (1) and (2) above can't give up on "correspondence," even if it might, following Rorty, dispense with representationalism.[37] I would suggest this doesn't quite go far enough—and doesn't adequately appreciate the pragmatist claim. For even "correspondence" language still tends to be held captive to what Taylor called the "inside/outside" (I/O) picture. And, as Taylor noted, "we can find the picture invoked within an argument that is meant to repudiate that very picture. This is what it means to be held captive."[38] If pragmatism is right about the contingent, social conditions of knowledge, then a Christian metaphysic (a sacramental ontology) not only has to be a realism without representation; it would also be a "realism" without correspondence. Or, to frame the point more carefully and with a little more nuance, we might put it this way: if pragmatism is right—that representation and correspondence and even "realism" are games that we learn to play from a community of social practice—then our realisms (and attendant claims to correspondence) are *dependent upon* communities of practice. In short, our claims about "reality" are *relative to* a community of social practice *and* the "environment" we inhabit.

My claim is not only that we *need* not choose between pragmatism and a sacramental ontology. It's stronger than that: ultimately we *can't* choose between the two of them, because to reject the pragmatist account of meaning and knowledge amounts to denying the finite, creaturely conditions of human knowledge. Now obviously one can be a pragmatist without affirming a sacramental ontology; but I would argue that one cannot affirm a sacramental ontology (or *any* ontology, for that matter) without being a "pragmatist" *insofar as* pragmatism is an account of the contingent, social conditions of human knowing. Any Christian

37. Ibid., 283. In *Truth in Aquinas*, Milbank and Pickstock also retain a commitment to truth as correspondence, but are at pains to point out that Thomas's participatory, illuminationist account of knowing involves a very different sort of correspondence from that assumed by Descartes, Locke, et al. (1–18). My concern is that their illuminationist account still doesn't recognize the *social* conditions of knowledge as pointed out by the pragmatist tradition.

38. Charles Taylor, "Merleau-Ponty and the Epistemological Picture," in *The Cambridge Companion to Merleau-Ponty*, ed. Taylor Carman and Mark B. N. Hansen (Cambridge: Cambridge University Press, 2005), 29.

account of creation and creaturehood (which a sacramental ontology is intended to be) will have to hew closely to something like pragmatism's account of contingency, dependence, and the social conditions of knowledge because these are simply our "best account" of features of creaturely finitude.[39] In this respect, Christian theology's relationship to pragmatism is akin to Augustine's relationship to Plato: because of the operations of "common grace," Christians can "loot the Egyptians," "stealing" Egyptian gold, as it were, to put it in service to the worship and glory of the Triune God.[40] I believe that the pragmatism of Wittgenstein, Rorty, and Brandom, while challenging some sedimented Christian habits of mind, actually offers a better account of the conditions of human creaturehood. In other words, pragmatism can teach us to be better theologians of creation and creaturehood, reminding us that at the heart of a Christian cosmology is a fundamental sense of the utter *dependence* of creation upon the Creator. Pragmatism is a prompt and ally in the much-needed work of articulating a Christian account of knowledge and meaning that takes seriously our contingency and sociality. Indeed, Rorty unwittingly reminds us of the beautiful, decentering truth that opens the Heidelberg Catechism: "That I am not my own. . . ."

So even our sacramental ontology is ultimately accounted for by the pragmatist account of knowledge. By "accounted for," I don't mean to suggest a reductionism, as if to "account for" a sacramental ontology is to "explain it away" in terms that reduce it to merely naturalistic causes. Rather, the point is that a sacramental ontology is itself a social and cultural *accomplishment*, dependent upon and relative to environmental conditions and a community of practice.[41] It is a "take" on reality, a construal of

39. On postfoundationalist, "best account" strategies of argument, see Charles Taylor, *Sources of the Self* (Cambridge, MA: Harvard University Press, 1989), 71–75.

40. "If those, however, who are called philosophers happen to have said anything that is true, and agreeable to our faith, the Platonists above all, not only should we not be afraid of them, but we should even claim back for our own use what they have said, as from its unjust possessors. It is like the Egyptians, who not only had idols and heavy burdens, which the people of Israel abominated and fled from, but also vessels and ornaments of gold and silver, and fine raiment, which the people secretly appropriated for their own, and indeed better, use as they went forth from Egypt." DC 2.40.60.

41. In language I'll introduce in the next chapter, after Brandom I would say that an ontology is a construal that operates in the "space of reasons."

the state of affairs within which we find ourselves. Those who are Christians take this to be *true*, and not just true "for them," but true *tout court*, as "the way things are." But this claim is made *from* a social location and is, in fact, dependent upon "trainings" received from a community of practice. If you're still hoping for a privileged representation that will provide a noncontingent *foundation* for the claims of a sacramental ontology (or any other aspect of Christian confession), then the pragmatist account is always going to feel "deflationary," like some kind of epistemic failure. But that just means you're haunted by Cartesian ghosts, confusing a misplaced quest for foundationalist certainty with truth and knowledge.[42] Again, as Rorty quipped, "We should not regret our inability to perform a feat which no one has any idea how to perform" (*PM*, 340). Which is just another way of saying we should not begrudge our finitude and creaturely contingency and despair that we can't achieve Godlike knowledge. We should not regret our inability to achieve something we were never made for. Foundationalist epistemologies and attempts to "secure" Christian confession by a mythical, noncontingent "correspondence" are nothing less than epistemologies of *in*dependence, which will always be inappropriate for (dependent) creatures.

We might say that the upshot of a pragmatist account of knowledge and truth is the simple but destabilizing recognition that, as knowers, we are always already *indebted* because we are contingent, dependent creatures.[43] And to be dependent is to be *gift*-ed. This is the fundamental status of the creature.[44] To be able to know is a social accomplishment made possible by *gifts*—from God,

42. Richard Bernstein famously referred to this as "Cartesian anxiety" in *Beyond Objectivism and Relativism: Science, Hermeneutics, and Praxis* (Philadelphia: University of Pennsylvania Press, 1983), 16–20.

43. God alone is *not* contingent—is *necessary* and *in*dependent. But *our* knowledge and confession of that truth is always and only the confession of creatures who are *essentially* contingent and finite. So truth that human beings could *say* could never be "absolute," absolved of all relation, since as creatures we are inherently relational and dependent. To pretend otherwise is to pre-tend to divinity. (This doesn't preclude the language of *theosis*, but it does mean that any "deification" of the creature is *always* going to be qualified as the deification of dependent creatures. Deification is not divinization.)

44. It is also why *gratitude* is the fundamental response called for *from* the creature. See Peter Leithart, *Gratitude: An Intellectual History* (Waco: Baylor University Press, 2013).

and from the others that God gives us. To construe the cosmos as created by the Triune God is to have *learned* to see it that way, which is to have been inculcated into a contingent community of practice. In Wittgensteinian terms, one is "trained" to know this because one has been gifted by a community that "talks this way," thus enabling us to *see* that way, to know the cosmos as such.

Does that mean we are just "making it up"? Does it mean that a sacramental ontology and a Christian understanding of the Triune God are just human inventions and bottom-up projections—something we "just learned" from other human beings? Doesn't the pragmatist account preclude divine revelation? No, on all counts. Instead, the pragmatist account helps us to understand the dynamics and conditions of revelation. Ultimately the Christian community is the community that "talks this way" because they have been encountered by the transcendent God, because they have received the gift of revelation from the One who incarnates himself for our sakes. As I have argued elsewhere, God's revelation to humanity is always condescensional: it meets us where we are in our contingency and dependence, gifted *to* human community and henceforth extended *through* human communities of practice.[45] "The people of God" is the name of a covenant community of social practice catalyzed by the gracious revelation of the transcendent Creator. But that revelation is always and only received insofar as it is a revelation under the conditions that we finite, dependent, contingent creatures *know*—insofar as the transcendent God condescends to speak into our "worldly" environment. God's revelation does not skyhook us out of our contingency and finitude; instead, God's revelation kenotically condescends *to* our contingency and finitude. This is perhaps the scandalous revelation about revelation that pragmatism compels us to recognize: that God's revelation is *contingent*, in at least two senses. First, God's act of revelation—like the act of creation—is not necessary, is not compelled, could have not been. God's self-revelation is free, and if it is "compelled," it is compelled only by God's love. Second, God's

---

45. On this "condescensional" logic of incarnation, see James K. A. Smith, *Speech and Theology: Language and the Logic of Incarnation*, Radical Orthodoxy Series (New York: Routledge, 2002); and James K. A. Smith, "Limited Inc/arnation: The Searle/ Derrida Debate Revisited in Christian Context," in *Hermeneutics at the Crossroads: Interpretation in Christian Perspective*, ed. Kevin Vanhoozer, James K. A. Smith, and Bruce Ellis Benson (Bloomington: Indiana University Press, 2006), 112–29.

revelation is contingent insofar as it is given *in time* to contingent beings. Any revelation that is going to be received *as* revelation by finite, temporal, social beings is a revelation that must be given under or into those conditions. And so God's self-revelation is contingent in the sense that it is *historical* and *particular*: given at particular times, in particular places, to particular people(s), culminating in the incarnation itself, in which God speaks "in Son" (Heb. 1:1–3) in the "fullness of time" (Gal. 4:4)—which is not some atemporal eternity but rather a contingent time, "under Pontius Pilate." That scandalously particular revelation is catalytic: through the regenerating and illuminating power of the Spirit it gathers a people, launches a tradition, and inaugurates a community of practice that is indebted to this revelation.

However, precisely because God's self-revelation is historical—in the incarnation, in the Word, in the people of God—that revelation is also now a feature of the "environment" with which humanity has to "cope." The revelation that undergirds Christian confession is now a "public" feature of the world with which humanity must grapple—part of the "obduracy" of reality, one of the "antics of things" that any and all humans have to "cope" with. Some, of course, will try to "cope" with this by writing it off, ignoring it, explaining it away. When Daniel Dennett or Richard Dawkins "write off" God's revelation, they are nonetheless contending with it in a sense. That is how they "cope" with this feature of our worldly environment with all of its history. But the wager of a Christian account of reality—and hence the wager of a pragmatist Christian "apologetic"—is that, in fact, any ontology or "final story" (as Rorty calls them) that doesn't receive this revelation *as* revelation is not going to be able to properly "cope" with the "pushback" of reality.[46] In other words, the Christian apologist will still make the case that Christian faith is the most "rational" response to these features of the (material, historical, cultural) environment

46. This is very much akin to Charles Taylor's "apologetic" in works such as *Sources of the Self* and *A Secular Age*, in which Taylor points to features of human experience (moral normativity in *Sources*; "fullness" in *A Secular Age*) that are best (and perhaps *only*) accounted for within a Christian framework. For relevant discussion, see Deane-Peter Baker, *Tayloring Reformed Epistemology: Charles Taylor, Alvin Plantinga, and the* de jure *Challenge to Christian Belief* (London: SCM, 2007); and James K. A. Smith, *How (Not) to Be Secular: Reading Charles Taylor* (Grand Rapids: Eerdmans, 2014).

that we inhabit, even though it will also concede that this account only "makes sense" when one is inculcated into the community of practice that is the church.[47]

To recognize the contingency of God's revelation is not to eviscerate its significance or "reduce" it to human invention. God reveals himself *to* and *in* and *under* these conditions; but it is the revelation *of* the transcendent, unconditioned, absolute Creator. In fact, the revelation of God received in the canon of the Scriptures reveals the contingent status of creation, but it is only revelation insofar as it is received *as* coming from the One we take to be noncontingent and absolute, who we confess is "God the Father Almighty." And yet one needs to "learn" to receive it as such, and the Spirit has elected to effect such "training" (in a Wittgensteinian sense) through the community of practice that is the body of Christ.[48] Everything we know and confess as Christians is *relative to* this (contingent, historical) revelation, and our reception of this *as* revelation is dependent upon our inculcation in the community of social practice that is the church. There is now no revelation outside the church because there is no meaning that is not "use."

Far from undercutting Christian orthodoxy, this simply brings us back to what we learned from Augustine in chapter 2: to see creation *as* creation, to receive the world as *sacramentum mundi*, depends upon (is relative to) a story *about* the world that is revealed to us by God and passed on to us in the community of the Spirit that is the church.[49] We might playfully suggest this amounts

47. We will further explore this notion of "rationality" in chap. 4.

48. In other words, the Spirit who regenerates and illumines us also condescends to the conditions of our dependence and sociality, inhabiting and working through the practices and artifacts of the body of Christ, the church. There could be no "magic" or "private" revelation to a contingent, dependent human creature that doesn't happen under the conditions described by a pragmatist account of meaning and knowledge.

49. This is also why a pragmatist account of knowledge and meaning—which I am arguing is the only account that really does justice to our contingency, dependence, and sociality—undercuts most accounts of "natural law" insofar as they treat natural law representationally—as something that can't be known atomistically, without dependence on a particular community of practice. Quite apart from a pragmatist critique on this point (but resonating with it), David Bentley Hart has recently pointed out the problems with such notions of natural law. As Hart puts it, like natural law theorists, "I certainly believe in a harmony between cosmic and moral order, sustained by the divine goodness in which both participate. I simply do not believe that the terms of that harmony are as precisely discernible as natural law thinkers imagine." The problem, then, is not the assertion that there are norms

to a nominalist account of Platonism—a pragmatist account of Christian realism. So a participatory ontology is itself given in a contingent tradition, in a distinct community of practice, operating according to the dynamics so well analyzed by the pragmatism of Wittgenstein, Rorty, and Brandom. To be part of this tradition— by the grace of God—is to be enabled to see the *truth* about the cosmos. But seeing this truth is *relative to* the story of God's self-revelation; being able to grasp this truth is *dependent upon* one's inculcation into the community of the Spirit. So it is not *either* truth *or* contingency; it's not that once we see the truth we magically escape the contingent communal conditions of knowing. Rather, we know *in* and *by* those conditions.

---

for human flourishing that are bound up with the "ends" of nature; the problem is that "the natural law theorist insists that the moral meaning of nature should be perfectly evident to any properly reasoning mind, *regardless of religious belief or cultural formation.*" David Bentley Hart, "Is, Ought, and Nature's Laws," *First Things*, March 2013, 72, emphasis added. What Hart calls "cultural formation" is what pragmatists like Wittgenstein and Rorty are getting at when they talk about social inculcation and "training"—learning with and from a community of practice how to "take" the world, how to "use" the world. "To put the matter very simply," Hart concludes, "belief in natural law is inseparable from the idea of nature as a realm shaped by final causes, oriented in their totality toward a single transcendent moral Good: one whose dictates cannot simply be deduced from our experience of the natural order, but must be received as an apocalyptic interruption of our ordinary explanations that nevertheless, miraculously, makes the natural order intelligible to us as a reality that opens up to what is more than natural." But such a "concept of nature . . . is *entirely dependent upon* supernatural (or at least metaphysical) convictions" (ibid., 71, emphasis added). And, the pragmatist account would add, one only comes by such convictions thanks to a community of practice that passes them on, in which one is trained to see the world in such a way. So the "recognition" of the moral *telos* of nature is *dependent upon* supernatural convictions that are *relative to* a particular community of revelation. Hence the pragmatist, *qua* pragmatist, does not deny the ontological reality of natural law; she or he only denies the possibility of *knowing* that law apart from membership in a contingent community of practice that teaches us to see the world as such. As Hart notes in his sequel to this piece ("Nature Loves to Hide," *First Things*, May 2013), at stake here is actually an account of the relationship between nature and grace. The Christian pragmatism I'm advocating would simply emphasize (per Rom. 1:21–23, but also per Calvin's account of the "book of nature" in the *Institutes*) that one needs to be inculcated in the community of *grace* that is the body of Christ in order to be able to "see" *nature* as the natural law theorist claims any rational being can. Oliver O'Donovan articulates a similar concern in *Resurrection and Moral Order: An Outline of Evangelical Ethics*, 2nd ed. (Grand Rapids: Eerdmans, 1994), 86–87. In chap. 4, in dialogue with Robert Brandom, we'll see that what's really at issue here is how to understand "rationality."

Herein lies a true epistemic humility that should not be confused with the false humility of skepticism. Skeptics aren't "humble" about their knowledge claims—because they don't have any! In our postmodern context, we too often confuse epistemic humility with *not knowing*. Such skepticism is usually the fruit of remaining captive to a foundationalist account of knowledge, the representationalist picture that holds us captive. To say "I don't know" is not really epistemically humble; it is simply a confession of ignorance (which can, of course, sometimes be a virtue). True epistemic humility would be more a matter of recognizing the contingency, dependence, and contestability of our claims while also unapologetically proclaiming them and seeking to convince others to see the world *our* way, precisely because we take them to be *true*.[50] It is just this sort of recognition that pragmatism fosters.[51] Such is the epistemic humility that should attend creaturely claims to knowledge.

---

50. On "deep" contestability that refuses bland "tolerance," see William E. Connolly, *Why I Am Not a Secularist* (Minneapolis: University of Minnesota Press, 1999), 8–10.

51. Rorty, of course, while holding to such a pragmatist account of knowledge and truth, was an unapologetic advocate for democracy and even American ideals. He described this advocacy as a kind of "ethnocentrism" (in "Solidarity or Objectivity?," in *Objectivity, Relativism, and Truth* [Cambridge: Cambridge University Press, 1991], 21–34). Some have latched on to this as a case of performative contradiction, as if Rorty's pragmatism should undercut any strong advocacy. But it is the criticism that fails to understand the nature of the pragmatist point.

4

Reasons to Believe

Making Faith Explicit after Brandom

Making Room for Reason(s): Brandom's Project

At its heart, the pragmatist tradition of Wittgenstein and Rorty is a philosophy of contingency—an account of meaning that (implicitly) recognizes our creational dependence. That appreciation of our dependence is bound up with an appreciation of our inextricably *social* condition: if meaning "depends," it's because *we* depend upon communities of practice who gift us with a world of meaning. Insofar as social dependence is a feature of being a creature, our social dependence is an effect of our dependence upon the Creator, who made us as such. This is why I've suggested that our epistemological desire to deny such dependence and contingency amounts to a hubristic denial of our very creaturehood—and *that* bears all the marks of our transgression in the garden. So, far from being the prerequisite for Christian orthodoxy, claims to "absolute" truth might be almost diabolical.

Both Wittgenstein and Rorty emphasized that what we receive from our contextual communities is, first and foremost, a kind of know-*how*: a way of being attuned to our world that is more like a tacit mastery of an environment than a logical, conceptual grasp of a proposition. Now, given the (corrective) emphases of both the later Wittgenstein and Rorty, it might seem that such an account is *anti*-propositional and anti-logical. But the growing corpus of their student and heir Robert Brandom demonstrates that these are not mutually exclusive—that appreciating meaning as use does not preclude a robust account of reason and logic, though it will require that we reconfigure our understanding of both. In taking up such a project, Brandom is kind of the "loyal opposition" of Wittgenstein and Rorty—dependent upon them, and in fundamental agreement that meaning is use, but taking that insight in different directions, at times directly critical of them. As such, his work represents a critical extension of the pragmatist tradition, and one that is of special interest for those interested in the relationship between Christian practice and Christian theology. We might think of Brandom as helping us to imagine a pragmatist theology—an account of how Christian doctrines and concepts (know-*what*) relate to Christian worship and practice (know-*how*).[1] So my goal is to offer an introduction to Brandom's project and then, in chapter 5, consider some of its implications for Christian theology. Since Brandom represents the "snowball" effect of pragmatism from Wittgenstein and Rorty, our final chapter will thereby tease out the theological implications of their work as well.

In his "big" book *Making It Explicit*, Brandom's opening question is disarmingly simple: "Who are 'we'?" The whole project hinges on that first-person plural pronoun. "For what we are is made as much as found, decided as well as discovered. The sort of thing we are depends, in part, on what we take ourselves to be."[2] The "we" Brandom is interested in is precisely the "we" who asks that question—the sorts of beings who express, articulate, and conceptualize such questions in order to understand who we are. So his project is introduced as a kind of philosophical ethnography or anthropology: what differentiates "us" from the animals is

---

1. In this respect, I see this chapter functioning as a supplement to my Cultural Liturgies project, further unpacking the final section of *Imagining the Kingdom*, entitled "Redeeming Reflection." I see Brandom offering resources to understand the dynamic, interactive relationship between Christian practice and theological articulation, while still granting a primacy and irreducibility to practice.

2. Robert Brandom, *Making It Explicit: Reasoning, Representing, and Discursive Commitment* (Cambridge, MA: Harvard University Press, 1994), 3. Before you over-read this claim, do note that qualifier: "in part."

precisely our ability to ask (and answer) such questions. The point of demarcation here isn't biological or physical; it is a distinction that is rooted in the ability of some beings to ask such questions.[3] It is this *ability* to ask and answer that makes us "us."

> What would have to be true—not only of the quaint folk across the river, but of chimpanzees, dolphins, gaseous extraterrestrials, or digital computers (things in many ways quite different from the rest of us)—for them nonetheless to be correctly counted among us? Putting the issue this way acknowledges an expansive demarcational commitment to avoid, as far as possible, requiring the sharing of adventitious stigmata of origin or material constitution. In understanding ourselves we should look to conditions at once more abstract and more practical, which concern what we are able to *do*, rather than where we come from or what we are made of.[4]

Now Brandom concedes that "each kind of 'we'-saying defines a different community, and we find ourselves in many communities." Sometimes "we" is the community of Americans, or the community of Christians, or the community of model railroad enthusiasts. Our "we"-sayings are always community specific. But Brandom "goes meta" with this insight: while there are many different communities, generating all sorts of different "we's," this phenomenological insight suggests that we could "think of ourselves in the broadest terms as the ones who say 'we.' It points to the one great Community comprising members of all particular communities—the Community of those who say 'we' with and to someone, whether the members of those different particular communities recognize each other or not."[5] This broadest possible Community is still demarcated, however. It doesn't include all animate beings, or even all those beings capable of engendering

---

3. And by demarcating in this way, Brandom actually leaves open the possibility that even, say, machines could become part of our "we" *if* they could exhibit the *capacities* he describes below. That would be the benchmark for artificial intelligence. For skepticism that this could ever be possible, see Hubert Dreyfus, *What Computers Still Can't Do: A Critique of Artificial Reason* (Cambridge, MA: MIT Press, 1992). As we'll see below, while this is a theoretical possibility, Brandom spends most of his time pointing out that machines (and animals) are the sorts of things *un*able to do this.

4. Brandom, *Making It Explicit*, 4.

5. Ibid.

"warm mammalian fellow-feeling." This "we" comprises those who can *say* "'we' *with* and *to* someone."[6]

Thus Brandom stipulates that "we" are those beings "distinguished by capacities that are broadly cognitive"; that is, our interactions with things and with one another "*mean* something to us, they have *conceptual content* for us, [and] we *understand* them in one way rather than another."[7] It is this capacity that demarcates us as "*reasonable* beings . . . ones on whom reasons are binding, who are subject to the peculiar force of the better reason,"[8] whereas "reason is as nothing to the beast of the field"; the beasts are neither bothered by evidence nor do they demand explanations. Only "we" are subject to that unique *normative* force of reason(s). To be rational is to be normed by reasons, subject to demands to explain ourselves.

So "we" are defined by what Brandom calls *sapience*, not mere *sentience*: "Sentience is what we share with non-verbal animals such as cats—the capacity to be *aware* in the sense of being *awake*. Sentience, an exclusively biological phenomenon insofar as our understanding yet reaches, is in turn to be distinguished from the mere reliable differential responsiveness we sentients share with artifacts such as thermostats and land mines."[9] Cats, humans, and land mines all react when touched; but land mines never go to sleep or are "aware" of predators in the neighborhood. So sentience is a kind of mid-level awareness characteristic of animals. But *sapience* distinguishes "us" even further: "Sapience concerns understanding or intelligence, rather than irritability or arousal. One is treating something as sapient insofar as one explains its behavior by attributing to it intentional states such as belief and desire as constituting reasons for that behavior."[10] In short, *sapient* beings—"us"—are those beings who can answer the question, "Why did you do that?"

What marks "us" out, then, is our capacity for reasoning—which is not, for Brandom, some capital-R "faculty" bequeathed to us as

6. Ibid. Brandom is very happy to own up to the Hegelian nature of his project (e.g., *Tales of the Mighty Dead: Historical Essays in the Metaphysics of Intentionality* [Cambridge, MA: Harvard University Press, 2002], 47–57). Recall Rorty's Hegelian concession: "The individual apart from his society is just one more animal" (*PM*, 192).

7. Brandom, *Making It Explicit*, 4.

8. Ibid., 5.

9. Ibid.

10. Ibid.

a built-in syllogistic mechanism from on high. Instead reason is a *capacity*, a unique set of capabilities forged as a social practice. To say "we" are rational is to emphasize that we give and take reasons. We ask questions and question motives. We ask whether and why we really need to be back in our dorm room by curfew; someone answers our question, gives us reasons that involve concepts; to this we might reply with different reasons and counter-concepts, or simply acquiesce as convinced. Rational beings are those unique animals who can have *arguments* because they can employ *concepts*.

Such reasoning is an accomplishment, a skill, a capacity honed in a community that is essentially linguistic.[11] For Brandom, dolphins and chimpanzees and other animals might be able to forge communities of social practice, and even cultivate a kind of know-*how* that could be said to be a rudimentary "culture." But what they don't do is talk; or more specifically, what they don't do is give and take reasons. They might even have systems of communication, but they don't have *language*—the unique instance of social practice that is discursive and conceptual. So Brandom's pragmatism shares Wittgenstein and Rorty's interest in communities of practice; but Brandom is specifically interested in language, "the social practices that distinguish us as rational, indeed logical, concept-mongering creatures."[12]

It is on just this point that Brandom is both an heir and critic of Wittgenstein and Rorty. In *Articulating Reasons*, one of the

11. This doesn't mean that we are *only* linguistic; the point is that what *distinguishes* humans as "rational" animals is our capacity to give and take reasons employing the currency of concepts. Brandom makes a similar point in a debate about Heidegger. The analysis of Dasein in *Being and Time* clearly accords priority to "practical" intentionality over "propositional" intentionality. However, Brandom argues that it is precisely propositional intentionality (thematization) that is *unique* to Dasein. "This is not to say that there cannot be norms implicit in social practices without norms explicit in the form of rules, which determine what is correct by saying or describing what is correct and, hence, without linguistic practices including assertion. It is to say that such a prelinguistic community would not count as Dasein" (*Tales of the Mighty Dead*, 329).

12. Brandom, *Making It Explicit*, xi. Brandom notes that one can get to the same demarcation by focusing on truth or agency: "We are believers, and believing is taking-true. We are agents, and acting is making-true. To be sapient is to have states such as belief, desire, and intention, which are contentful in the sense that the question can appropriately be raised under what circumstances what is believed, desired, or intended would be *true*. Understanding such a content is grasping the conditions necessary and sufficient for its truth" (ibid., 5).

more accessible entrées into Brandom's corpus (and on which I'll focus in this chapter), he notes that we can distinguish accounts of meaning based on whether or not they emphasize this difference between human, rational animals and other social species. The litmus test is "the relative priority accorded to *continuities* and *dis*continuities between discursive and nondiscursive creatures: the similarities and differences between the judgments and actions of concept users, on the one hand, and the uptake of environmental information and instrumental interventions of non-concept-using organisms and artifacts, on the other."[13] Some philosophers try to make sense of human meaning making and linguistic practices by emphasizing how much linguistic practices are *like* nondiscursive practices—how language use grows out of more basic, pre-linguistic practices of "coping" that we might also share with animals. Brandom describes these as "assimilation" accounts—assimilating the distinctly human social practice of language to wider social practices that are shared with other creatures. And he associates this assimilationist account with "the classical American pragmatists, and perhaps . . . the later Wittgenstein" (*AR*, 3)—a claim that would seem confirmed by our expositions of them in earlier chapters.[14]

In contrast to such assimilationist approaches that emphasize continuity (and sort of reduce linguistic practice *to* nondiscursive practice), Brandom emphasizes *dis*continuities. "I am more interested," he says, "in what separates concept users from non-concept users than in what unites them" (3). Thus his project is "differentiationist" (2). Linguistic practices are a specific set of social practices more broadly; but they are also distinct and irreducible—they are *not* "just like" other practices. They are unique, and uniquely human.

13. Robert Brandom, *Articulating Reasons: An Introduction to Inferentialism* (Cambridge, MA: Harvard University Press, 2000), 2–3; henceforth abbreviated in the text as *AR*.

14. Later he includes Heidegger in this "conceptual assimilationism," and contrasts this approach with the "*rationalist* pragmatism" of Hegel (*AR*, 34). However, in another study of Heidegger, Brandom argues that contrary to assimilationist readings of Heidegger (from Dreyfus, Haugeland, and Okrent), in fact Heidegger might also be described as a "rationalist pragmatist" insofar as Dasein is the being who thematizes. See Brandom, "Dasein, the Being That Thematizes," in *Tales of the Mighty Dead*, 325–47.

Brandom emphasizes that *both* aspects are true, and even if different projects have a different emphasis, both approaches need to account for continuities *and* discontinuities.

> Of course, wherever the story starts, it will need to account both for the ways in which concept use is like the comportments of nondiscursive creatures and the ways in which it differs. Theories that *assimilate* conceptually structured activity to the nonconceptual activity out of which it arises (in evolutionary, historical, and individual-development terms) are in danger of failing to make enough of the difference. Theories that adopt the converse strategy [like Brandom's], addressing themselves at the outset to what is *distinctive* of or exceptional about the conceptual, court the danger of not doing justice to generic similarities. (*AR*, 3)

My project so far, echoing Wittgenstein and Rorty, has been more assimilationist precisely because I think Christian theology and philosophy have tended to think of meaning in an *overly* conceptual manner that fails to appreciate the *con*tinuities between discursive practice and social practices more broadly. In that respect, a lot of Christian philosophy (and "folk" philosophy in the pews and apologetics programs) has failed Brandom's continuity test by failing to recognize that meaning is use. So the pragmatist emphasis on continuity in Wittgenstein and Rorty is salutary and corrective. But now having appreciated that, Brandom offers a helpful corrective to the corrective—an invitation to now re-appreciate (and freshly articulate) what is distinctive about human reasoning. In doing so, I believe Brandom offers us a framework to reconceive Christian theology in a way that accords with pragmatist insights about the creational conditions of contingency and community.

Making It Explicit

Brandom describes his project as either a "conceptual pragmatism" (*AR*, 4) or a "rationalist pragmatism" (10). If we can understand these descriptions, we'll have a platform to dive into the particulars. The account is *pragmatist* because it is still focused on *practice*; it is *conceptual* or *rationalist* because it is focused on those unique discursive and conceptual practices that constitute *rationality* or "sapience." It is a conceptual pragmatism because he sees the latter

growing out of—and dependent upon—the former. While Brandom
will emphasize what is distinctive about linguistic and conceptual practices, he still sees our linguistic practice as a species of
social practices more broadly. This is what he calls a "pragmatist
direction of explanation," in contrast to "a *platonist* strategy." A
platonist strategy is top-down: it thinks concepts come first, like
innate ideas planted in the mind, which then get "used" or "applied" in practice. This is just the sort of picture that Wittgenstein
has called into question, and Brandom follows him on this score.
Thus Brandom's pragmatist explanation "seeks to explain how the
use of linguistic expressions, or the functional role of intentional
states, confers conceptual content on them" (4). Concepts, then,
sort of bubble-up from the wider web of our social practices and
"skillful doings": conceptual content is something "conferred" on
our linguistic givings-and-takings. Concept using is a distinctly
sapiential form of use, but also one that assumes "the background
of various other kinds of skillful doing" (2). So meaning is use, but
conceptual meaning—the unique sort of meaning in which "we"
traffic—is a distinctive kind of use, even though it is also one that
assumes a wider web of (nonconceptual) social practices.

Summarizing his project, Brandom says that his conceptual
pragmatism

> offers an account of knowing (or believing, or saying) *that* such and
> such is the case in terms of knowing *how* (being able) to *do* some-
> thing. It approaches the contents of conceptually *explicit* proposi-
> tions or principles from the direction of what is *implicit* in practices
> of using expressions and acquiring and deploying beliefs. . . . The
> sort of pragmatism adopted here seeks to explain what is assert*ed*
> by appeal to features of assert*ings*, what is claim*ed* in terms of
> claim*ings*, what is judg*ed* by judg*ings*, and what is believ*ed* by
> the role of believ*ings* (indeed, what is expressed by express*ings* of
> it)—in general, the content by the act, rather than the other way
> around. (*AR*, 4)

Embedded in this dense summary are two important "frames"
for understanding Brandom's project. First, notice the distinction
and relation between knowing-*that* and knowing-*how*. Brandom
is a pragmatist because he emphasizes the priority of know-*how*.
Know-how (the sort of tacit mastery and competence emphasized
by Wittgenstein) precedes knowing-that (the sort of conceptual,

propositional formulations that we usually associate with "knowl-edge"). As Wittgenstein put it, you might be a master of the game without knowing how to articulate the rules. There is a kind of understanding or know-how that is characteristic of social prac-tices—of "coping," as Rorty puts it. But Brandom is interested in the unique subset of social practices that are conceptual and linguistic; and *those* practices, he claims, are knowings-*that*, which grow out of—and are dependent upon—our prior know-how.[15] These are still *practices*, but of a distinct sort.

This relation is at the heart of the second way he frames his project. Notice in the quote above that the relationship between (nondiscursive) know-*how* and (discursive) know-*that* is a rela-tion between what is *implicit* and what is made *explicit*.[16] The "content" articulated in concepts and propositions is a way of making explicit what is implicit in our prediscursive know-how. Concepts (which are linguistic) are the way we *talk* about what we *do*—and hence we can question *why* we're doing X, and give reasons in reply. Concept-using creatures ("concept-mongering creatures," as Brandom memorably puts it) are those beings who not only *do*—not only "practice"—but are also accountable for what they do, give reasons for what they do, and ask for reasons for what others do. As we'll see shortly, this aspect of account-ability and responsibility is central to Brandom's account. But for now we need to appreciate that such conceptual formulation is the making explicit of what was implicit in our practices—articulating as know-*that* what was previously only know-*how*.

What distinguishes Brandom's "rationalist" pragmatism from the pragmatism of Dewey, Wittgenstein, and Rorty is his interest in this unique "plane" of linguistic and conceptual practice that emerges only for concept-mongering creatures like us. He doesn't deny that this is rooted in a wider web of social practices—in the implicit know-how of a community of practice; it's just that he's interested in what makes "us" unique, which he locates in the move from implicit to explicit, from know-how to know-that. And only "we" (*sapient* creatures) can "make explicit."

The point of difference can be further refined, taking us back to a metaphor introduced by Wittgenstein. In *Philosophical*

---

15. In other words, "semantics is rooted in pragmatics" (*Making It Explicit*, 649).
16. Recall the title of Brandom's earlier systematic book: *Making It Explicit*.

Investigations, §18, Wittgenstein suggested that "our language can be seen as an ancient city": it is a motley, compiled over the ages, "a maze of little streets and squares," with no defined "downtown." In contrast, Brandom emphasizes that his "rationalist" pragmatism departs from Wittgenstein on just this point: "Such a view [i.e., Brandom's] entails that practices of giving and asking for reasons have a privileged, indeed defining, role with respect to linguistic practice generally" (*AR*, 14). In other words, contra Wittgenstein, there *is* a "center" of linguistic practice, and it is conceptual inference.

> Thus the "Slab" *Sprachspiel* [language-game] that Wittgenstein introduces in the opening sections of the *Philosophical Investigations* should not, by these standards of demarcation, count as a genuine *Sprach*spiel. It is a *vocal* but not yet a *verbal* practice. By contrast to Wittgenstein, the *inferential* identification of the conceptual [Brandom's view] claims that language (discursive practice) has a *center*; it is not a motley. Inferential practices of producing and consuming *reasons* are *downtown* in the region of linguistic practice. Suburban linguistic practices utilize and depend on the conceptual contents forged in the game of giving and asking for reasons, are parasitic on it. (*AR*, 14, emphases added)

Now, we need to be careful not to misunderstand Brandom's claim here. He is not suggesting that conceptual inference is primary *en toto* or *simpliciter*, as if he were claiming that know-what precedes know-how. His whole model is invested in recognizing the primacy of nonlinguistic social practices, the primacy of know-how to know-that. He reiterates this in *Between Saying and Doing*.

> A pragmatist line of thought common to the Dewey of *Experience and Nature* and *Art as Experience*, the Heidegger of *Being and Time*, and the Wittgenstein of the *Philosophical Investigations* is that there is such a thing as hermeneutic understanding in this sense, it is a genuine and distinctive kind of understanding, and it is the most basic kind of understanding, in the sense that all other sorts of understanding are parasitic on it and develop out of it. It is the primordial sort of practical discursive know-how: the capacity to engage in an autonomous discursive practice. In particular, they are concerned to insist that the sort of algebraic understanding characteristic of mature mathematized sciences—the sort for which analytic philosophers long—is pragmatically dependent . . .

on everyday hermeneutic understanding, which accordingly cannot be replaced by, or reduced to, the more technical kind. I accept all of these pragmatist claims about the distinctiveness and basicness or ordinary hermeneutic understanding of discursive performances and their products.[17]

So his claim about a rational "center" of language is more specific: he is suggesting that when it comes to *linguistic* practice, giving and asking for *reasons* is central, privileged, and somehow primary. But this concept-centrism seems to me both contestable and not a *necessary* feature of Brandom's model. It seems contestable because one could locate instances of language use that are not primarily defined by, nor dependent upon, propositional content or inference. Concrete poetry comes to mind; does Brandom want to commit himself to claiming that such poetry is not "linguistic?"[18] But more importantly, I don't see Brandom's "downtown" claim as an essential feature of his rationalist pragmatism. One could accept his account of the relationship between know-how and know-what, and even adopt his unique account of inference, without having to make the further claim that all other linguistic practices are "parasitic" upon conceptual practices.[19] In any case, we need not agree with Brandom about his "center" claim in order to appreciate and appropriate his pragmatist account of what's unique about *conceptual* practices.

This brings us to two more key features of Brandom's model: *expression* and *inference*. Brandom describes his project as an "expressivism" because that's how he sees the move from implicit to explicit, from know-how to know-that.[20] Conceptual content

17. Robert Brandom, *Between Saying and Doing* (Oxford: Oxford University Press, 2008), 212–13. It should be noted that this is in the context of Brandom arguing that, nonetheless, the "analytic project" is *not* thereby discredited as such.

18. He may retort that such uses are "vocal" but not yet "verbal," as with the "Slab!" *Sprachspiel*.

19. In a way, this recalls the debate between Jacques Derrida and John Searle about the primacy of metaphor. (Searle suggested that metaphor was always parasitic upon the literal, which Derrida contested.) For a discussion, see James K. A. Smith, "Limited Inc/arnation: The Searle/Derrida Debate Revisited in Christian Context," *Hermeneutics at the Crossroads: Interpretation in Christian Perspective*, ed. Kevin Vanhoozer, James K. A. Smith, and Bruce Ellis Benson (Bloomington: Indiana University Press, 2006), 112–29.

20. Brandom notes both his debts to, and distance from, the Romantic notions of "expression" associated with Herder et al. (*AR*, 8).

does not "represent"—and therefore conform to—some "outside" reality. Concepts are not interior puzzle pieces that "fit" some external reality. Like both Wittgenstein and Rorty, Brandom rejects this inside/outside picture and the representationalism that goes with it. Instead, building on what we just noted, Brandom argues that conceptual content *expresses* (i.e., makes explicit) the commitments that are implicit in our practices. So this isn't expression in the Romantic sense of "transforming what is inner into what is outer" (*AR*, 8); that would still be to accept the I/O picture. Instead, we should think of expression as "making *explicit* what is *implicit*. This can be understood in the pragmatist sense of turning something we can initially only *do* into something we can *say*: codifying some sort of knowing *how* in the form of a knowing *that*" (*AR*, 8). "We" are those creatures who can turn what we *do* into something that we *say*. And because we can do that, we can also ask, "Why did you do that?" To answer that question is to give reasons, which requires the deployment of concepts.[21] "Expressing something is *conceptualizing* it: putting it into conceptual form" (*AR*, 16).

This leads to Brandom's other key theme: *inference*. "The master idea that animates and orients this enterprise," he says, "is that what distinguishes specifically *discursive* practices from the doings of non-concept-using creatures is their *inferential* articulation" (*AR*, 10–11). Concept-mongering creatures not only *say*; they are responsible for what they say—and they are the unique sorts of discursive creatures who are responsible for how what they say fits within a web of implication and inference. In a dense but crucial passage, Brandom explains that to make something explicit in discursive practice amounts to

> putting it in a form in which it can both serve as and stand in need of *reasons*: a form in which it can serve as both premise and conclusion in *inferences*. Saying or thinking *that* things are thus-and-so is undertaking a distinctive kind of *inferentially* articulated

21. As we'll discuss further below, Brandom also sketches an expressivist understanding of logic: "Logic is not properly understood as the study of a distinctive kind of *formal* inference. It is rather the study of the inferential roles of vocabulary playing a distinctive *expressive* role: codifying in explicit form the inferences that are implicit in the use of ordinary, nonlogical vocabulary" (*AR*, 30). This will become clearer after we understand what Brandom means by inference.

commitment: putting it forward as a fit premise for further inferences, that is, *authorizing* its use as such a premise, and undertaking *responsibility* to entitle oneself to that commitment, to vindicate one's authority, under suitable circumstances, paradigmatically by exhibiting it as the conclusion of an inference from other such commitments to which one is or can become entitled. Grasping the *concept* that is applied in such a making explicit is mastering its *inferential* use: knowing (in the practical sense of being able to distinguish, a kind of knowing *how*) what else one would be committing oneself to by applying the concept, what would entitle one to do so, and what would preclude such entitlement. (*AR*, 11)

To appreciate Brandom's point, read that passage again and note the normative, almost "moral" language, that he uses: *undertaking*, *commitment*, *authorizing*, *responsibility*, *vindicate*. To *say* something—to *use* a concept—is, in a sense, to assert one's citizenship in the discursive community of concept users. That comes with certain rights and privileges, you might say, but it also comes with responsibilities. If you say the bottle on the table is blue, and we come to an agreement on that use of the concept, then I'm going to hold you responsible for "knowing" that it is not green. To say it is "blue" is to effectively *commit* yourself to that. And to commit yourself to that claim is to also (inferentially) commit yourself to some assumptions and entailments that are bound up with that (e.g., that the bottle is not red or pink or fuschia; that the bottle is not invisible; that this blue thing is a bottle and not a milk jug, etc., etc.). The concepts "blue" and "bottle" are nodes within a complex conceptual web, and competent citizens of the concept-using community are held responsible for those inferences. We'll explore this point in more detail below. For now, the upshot is to recognize that concept using—which is to move from the implicit to the explicit—is a *normative* game: there are rules to follow. To be rational is to be willing and able to play by the rules of the inferential game.

"Inferentialism" is a "use" theory of meaning that sees conceptual meaning as primarily *relational* (*AR*, 9)—not in the mushy sense of merely being intersubjective, but rather in the sense that meaning is bound up with a web of implications that are the "explicitations" of our know-*how*. Indeed, we might think of Brandom as teasing out the implications of Rorty's provocative claim that "truth is what your peers will let you get away with saying";

it's just that Brandom emphasizes that "our" peers are concept users, and "our" community of practice is one that is characterized by mastery of *inference*. In the next chapter we will explore the implications of this for the Christian "logic" that is theology. But first we need to drill down into particular aspects of Brandom's account, which I've only sketched in outline so far.

Content Matters: Inference and the Ethics of Language

When Brandom emphasizes that his conceptual pragmatist account of meaning is bound up with *in*ference, we should hear this as an alternative to *ref*erence. In this sense, he extends the critique of referentialism and representationalism we first heard in Wittgenstein and Rorty. But now Brandom can further help us to see why giving up on referentialism does not mean giving up on truth (though we also saw hints of how that could be the case in Rorty). If we are going to take seriously the contingency and communal nature of our knowledge, then we need to locate the dynamics of truth in inference, not reference.[22]

We first need to get an expansive sense of what counts as a "concept"; otherwise we're going to be tempted to imagine concepts as highly specialized, technical terms that we employ in long syllogisms. In that case, we'll mistakenly think that "concepts" are the sorts of odd things you only bump into at universities and philosophy conferences, not in "everyday life" at the coffee shop or on the playground or at church.

But in fact, for Brandom, concepts are quite ho-hum, everyday tools that "we" use all the time. Just to say "This ball is red" is to deploy concepts; so you can imagine the young child being welcomed into concept using as she begins to learn how to use the words "red" and "ball." Granted, this is still quite a unique notion of "concepts." If I simply report, "This ball is red," I'm not trying to make an argument; the claim is not a premise in a syllogism,

---

22. Brandom suggests that this is the more interesting way to demarcate schools of thought in modern philosophy (Descartes through Kant). Instead of carving them up into empiricists vs. rationalists, it would be more illuminating to contrast "the still dominant tradition that reads inferential correctness off from representational correctness" (*AR*, 46–47) with a minority report of those who invert this relationship. That alternative tradition would ultimately give us Hegel.

and so it wouldn't seem to be "inferential" in any sense—it doesn't seem to be part of any logical "chain." However, Brandom will emphasize that *if* this is a report made by a concept user, then "even such noninferential reports must be inferentially articulated" (*AR*, 47). Otherwise, we wouldn't be able to "tell the difference between noninferential reporters and automatic machinery such as thermostats and photocells, which also have reliable dispositions to respond differentially to stimuli" (47–48). We can train parrots or build sensors that could effectively report "This ball is red" when properly stimulated or affected (that is, we can design them to respond differentially to relevant stimuli—in this case, spherical red objects). But their vocalizations would not be *conceptual* precisely because those "reports" are not something for which they would be held *responsible*. In short, "The thermostat and the parrot do not understand their responses, those responses mean nothing to them, though they can mean something to us" (48). Thermostats, parrots, and humans might all be able to "classify" an object as a ball and as red, but only the concept-using human grasps the *implications* of saying "The ball is red" when she makes that report.

So what makes the report "This ball is red" conceptual? It is the reporter's practical mastery of all the inferences that are bound up with that claim. Following Wilfrid Sellars, Brandom encapsulates his point this way:

> For a response to have *conceptual* content is just for it to play a role in the *inferential* game of making claims and giving and asking for reasons. To grasp or understand such a concept is to have practical mastery over the inferences it is involved in—to know, in the practical sense of being able to distinguish (a kind of know-*how*), what follows from the applicability of a concept, and what it follows from. The parrot does not treat "That's red" as incompatible with "That's green," nor as following from "That's scarlet" and entailing "That's colored." Insofar as the repeatable response is not, for the parrot, caught up in practical proprieties of inference and justification, and so of the making of further judgments, it is not a *conceptual* or *cognitive* matter at all. (*AR*, 48)

Only concept users like you and me are masters of the web of implications that are bound up with the simple report that "This ball is red." Many of the inferences packed into this claim will remain implicit; but we know *how* to manage them if asked, and we functionally assume them when we make the report. We are practical masters of the fact that we shouldn't call red balls green, or call red balls red shoes.[23] To understand that the claim "This ball is red" is incompatible with "This ball is purple" is to *grasp a concept*, which is to grasp what can and cannot be *inferred* from that claim. Your parrot or thermostat is never going to do that.

The next question we should ask is, What is the *source* of such inferences? What governs good inferences, and what distinguishes good from bad inferences? *Why* is it that "This ball is red" is incompatible with "This ball is green," but *not* incompatible with "This ball is scarlet"? Whence the *rules* of inference?

This is where we'll be tempted to fall back into a "platonist" account (as Brandom calls it), or to revert to *reference* in order to explain *in*ference. "Well," someone might answer, "of course the claim that the ball is red is incompatible with the claim that the ball is green because the former *corresponds* to the relevant state of affairs whereas the latter does not." That sort of move would root inference in reference, and would locate justification in correspondence. But on this point, Brandom (following Wittgenstein, Sellars, and Rorty) is an unapologetic pragmatist, for all of the reasons we laid out in chapters 2 and 3. Justification is fundamentally *social*. So inference is not rooted in reference; to the contrary, reference is one kind of *in*ferential game we can play, and ultimately what counts as a good inference is bound up with a community of know-*how*, a community of practice. As we'll see in a moment, this does *not* mean we can get way with just inventing rules of inference. But first we need to appreciate a key distinction Brandom emphasizes.

Brandom is talking about what he calls *material* inference, rather than the sort of "formal" rules of inference that we normally associate with logical analysis. Think of the distinction this way: "formal" rules of inference are associated with what we usually call *validity*. Reasoning and inference is described as "valid" when the *form* of the inference conforms to what are taken to be universal rules of logic (like the law of the excluded middle), abstracted from

---

23. This is why Brandom also emphasizes that "in order to master *any* concept, one must master *many* concepts. For grasp of one concept consists in mastery of at least some of its inferential relations to other concepts. Cognitively, grasp of just one concept is the sound of one hand clapping" (*AR*, 49). This echoes both Wittgenstein's and Rorty's "holism."

any particular content. So, for example, the following syllogism would be considered "valid" and hence the conclusion would be a "good (formal) inference":

1. All unicorns have a single spiraled horn.
2. Bob Brandom is a unicorn.
3. Therefore, Bob Brandom has a single spiraled horn.

Now, I've never met Professor Brandom in person, and while his author photo sports a very impressive ZZ Top–like beard, I'm quite confident that he is not a unicorn. So while the above conceptual constellation conforms to rules of *formal* inference, this is not the kind of inference that interests Brandom.[24]

"Material" inferences, in contrast, are rules of inference that are bound up with the specific *matter* at hand. They are inferences that are bound up with, and dependent upon, the specific *content* of the concepts at issue. Consider examples like

> the inference from "Pittsburgh is to the west of Princeton" to "Princeton is to the east of Pittsburgh," and that from "Lightning is seen now" to "Thunder will be heard soon." It is the contents of the concepts *west* and *east* that make the first a good inference, and the contents of the concepts *lightning* and *thunder*, as well as the temporal concepts, that make the second appropriate. Endorsing these inferences is part of grasping or mastering those concepts, quite apart from any specifically *logical* competence. (*AR*, 52)

What counts as a good (material) inference cannot be separated from familiarity with material realities, like where Pittsburgh is, where Princeton is, what lightning is, and how it relates to thunder. The *truth* of such inferences is not the sort that can be abstractly and formally reduced to P's and Q's in some universal syllogism. The Pittsburgh/Princeton case also highlights how *contingent* and *historical* such material inferences are, dependent on the contingency of historical entities and a concrete know-how regarding the *matters* at hand. The truth of such inferences is dependent upon the contingent, historical settlement of Pittsburgh and Princeton.

24. Furthermore, Brandom does not think that such formal reference is either primary or governing.

The rules of material inference are bottom-up, not top-down. They don't fall from some logical heaven, nor are they handed down from some Supremely Rational Being as veritable revelations to which our reasoning must conform. Instead, inferences that matter bubble *up* in two senses: On the one hand, they are material inferences that are constrained by matter, by the material conditions we inhabit—what Rorty called the "obduracy" of the things we bump into. On the other hand, these rules of inference are forged by the community of concept-mongering creatures, bubbling up from the know-how we've acquired coping with these material conditions. It's because "we" have inhabited these material conditions that the concepts of "thunder" and "lightning" emerged, and it's because of specific, obdurate material conditions that the rules of *good* inference about lightning and thunder have emerged. And now we hold one another *responsible* for making *good* inferences about thunder and lightning.

So Brandom's "rationalism" is not a rationalism "from above," as it were—as if it were a "platonism." Rather his is a rationalism "from below": "we" are rational because we are able to make explicit these material inferences that are carried in the concepts that *express* our know-how. And because of that, we are *responsible* for what we say—accountable to one another, part of a community of concept users who, at any moment, can ask us to give *reasons* for what we say.[25] The rules of inference emerge from the specificity of a community's discursive practices.

What "makes (inferential) sense" depends on the conceptual content that is conferred by the relevant discursive community. In short, when it comes to what counts as good inference, *it depends*. It depends on material conditions, *and* it depends on being acculturated to a community of concept users, thereby absorbing the rules that govern good inference. This brings us back to a key emphasis in Wittgenstein: we have to *learn* meaning. We have to be trained in language-games, in the discursive communities that are home to the rules of inference. If "asserting a sentence is implicitly undertaking a commitment to the correctness of the material inference from

---

25. One of the more intriguing aspects of Brandom's project is his suggestion that logic is *expressive*—the formal articulation of the inferences that we know *how* to manage in our practice. (He also suggests that an argument to this effect is already implicit in Frege; see *AR*, 57–61.) In some ways, one could read *Between Saying and Doing* as his elucidation of this intuition.

its circumstances to its consequences of application," then I, as a sentence maker and concept user, need to be taught the rules that govern "correctness" (*AR*, 63). This is not a matter of matching up a mythical "inside" with an "outside"; rather, it's a matter of absorbing a mastery of these material inferences. This should *not* be thought of representationally as

> the turning on of a Cartesian light, but as practical mastery of a certain kind of inferentially articulated doing: responding differentially according to the circumstances of proper application of a concept, and distinguishing the proper inferential consequences of such application. . . . Thinking clearly is on this inferentialist rendering a matter of knowing what one is committing oneself to by a certain claim, and what would entitle one to that commitment. (*AR*, 63–64)

So even our conceptual life requires the absorption of a know-how, and we effectively become citizens of this kingdom of conceptual understanding when we are able and willing to take responsibility for what we say. Competent concept users know how to responsibly manage the inferences that are loaded into concepts. And they are able to do so both "forward" and "backward," you might say; that is, I grasp a concept when I understand both how it could be a premise and how it could be a conclusion—how it follows from some things and entails/implies others.

What this means, quite baldly, is that in some significant sense "rationality" is relative because the rules governing *good* inference are also relative: to material conditions and to a community of discursive practice. *And we human concept mongerers are always already immersed in both*. We are never *not* inhabitants of an environment of material conditions; and we are never *not* members of a community of discursive practice. Indeed, these are just the *conditions of creaturehood*. Furthermore, almost all of the truths of the Christian faith—rooted in the history of the people of God, the incarnation, death, and resurrection of Jesus—are truths of the same sort. The truth of Christianity is the (contingent) truth of material inference, not platonic deduction.

This is why the disclosure of a supposedly universal logic of validity does not necessarily help us make sense of all sorts of inferences that we count as *good* inferences. It is not conformity to formal rules of validity that makes inferences good or true; to the contrary, the *formal* goodness of inferences derives from and is explained in terms of the *material* goodness of inferences (*AR*, 55). Interestingly, Brandom picks out "*the*ological (or aesthetic) vocabulary" as a case in point (55): what "makes sense" theologically or aesthetically is inextricably linked to concrete, material conditions. One would need to be inducted into relevant communities of practice in order to understand what counts as "rational" in such discursive universes because the material content of these communities matters when it comes to determining what is "rational"—what constitutes a "good move" in *this* particular language-game. In short, "rationality" *depends*.

Conceptual articulation helps us "make explicit" the inferences that are often left implicit in our know-how as competent linguistic practitioners. To be part of a community of linguistic practice is to know how to manage inference without usually having to talk about it. However, to be concept users is to be the sort of creatures who *can* make these inferences explicit.

But *why* should we want to make such inferences explicit? What's the point of converting our know-how into know-that? If we are competent concept users, we are usually doing this *implicitly*; isn't that enough? As Brandom sees it, the virtue of making our implicit know-how explicit is that it enables us to see inconsistencies where we might not have otherwise. Conceptual articulation and clarification can then serve to hone our inferential sense. "We want to be aware of the inferential commitments our concepts involve, to be able to make them explicit, and to be able to justify them" (*AR*, 72). Following Sellars once again, Brandom sees this as the heart of the Socratic method: "Socratic method is a way of bringing our practices under rational control by expressing them explicitly in a form in which they can be confronted with objections and alternatives" (*AR*, 56)—though such objections and alternatives are also constrained by material conditions. Only when we make them explicit can we begin to discern inconsistencies and seek to harmonize our commitments, which is a feature of being "rational." "The expressive task of making material inferential commitments explicit plays an essential role in the reflectively rational Socratic practice of harmonizing our commitments" (*AR*, 76).

This takes us back to language we encountered earlier. For Brandom, just by speaking I already functionally take up an *ethical*

stance: "Asserting a sentence is implicitly undertaking a commitment" (*AR*, 63). Others in the community of practice are going to
hold me *responsible* for the inferences that are bound up with that
sentence; they can demand reasons from me to justify my claim;
they can hold me accountable for the implications of my claim;
they can justifiably fault me for holding contradictory claims; and
so on. To be a concept user is to inhabit a *normative* space.

To recognize this is just to grant our indebtedness to Kant,
"the great, gray mother of us all" (*AR*, 80). When Brandom distinguishes sentience from sapience—distinguishes parrots from
people—he is echoing "Kant's big idea," that

> what distinguishes judgment and action from the responses of
> merely natural creatures is neither their relation to some special
> stuff nor their peculiar transparency, but rather that they [i.e., judg-
> ment and action] are what we are in a distinctive way *responsible*
> for. They express *commitments* of ours: commitments that we are
> answerable for in the sense that our *entitlement* to them is always
> potentially at issue; commitments that are *rational* in the sense that
> vindicating the corresponding entitlements is a matter of offering
> *reasons* for them. (*AR*, 80)

Again, it's not too much of a stretch to see this as Brandom's
gloss on that provocative Rortyan quip that "truth is what your
friends will let you get away with saying." But Brandom shows
that this is *not* a license for *ir*responsibility; to the contrary,
linguistic practice is inherently *normative*. Using concepts is a
practice for which we are held responsible. Indeed, it's ironic
that some hear Rorty's quip as if it granted license for us to say
whatever we want, when in fact the very opposite is the case: we
are held responsible by a community. Hence "the rationality that
qualifies us as *sapients* (and not merely sentients) can be identified with being a player in the social, implicitly normative game
of offering and assessing, producing and consuming, reasons"
(*AR*, 81).[26] "We" are those who inhabit "the space of reasons,"

---

26. Brandom goes on to describe discursive practice as "deontic scorekeeping":
"The significance of a speech act is how it changes what commitments and entitlements one attributes and acknowledges" (*AR*, 81). I think one could legitimately
question whether all speech acts are moves that try to "win," but I won't pursue
the point here.

and in that space we express (make explicit) what was implicit in our practice and hold one another accountable to the inferences assumed therein. It is these sorts of obligations that bind us to one another. Such are the obligations of being rational. Far from being oppressive constraints, they free us to be human, to be social, to be *with*.

"Making It Explicit" in *I've Loved You So Long*

Some things need to be said. This is one of the upshots of Brandom's expressivist inferentialism. While the pragmatist tradition helps us appreciate how meaning is often *wider* than language, Brandom's "rationalist" pragmatism also emphasizes our unique ability to conceptually articulate our commitments—and the *ethical* import of doing so. It's only once—and because—we are able to make explicit our assumptions and commitments that we can also ask, "Why did you do that?" And we are the sorts of creatures who have a responsibility to answer that question. We are subject to the demand to *explain* ourselves. Our tacit know-how needs to be expressed in conceptual articulation in the space of reasons. That's what it means to be "rational."

This demand—this *need*—for expression, articulation, and explanation is illustrated in Philippe Claudel's (very![27]) French film *I've Loved You So Long*, with stunning, understated performances by Kristen Scott Thomas (Juliette) and Elsa Zylberstein (Léa). The story explores the dynamics of silence and speech, community and isolation, dependence and detachment, and above all the demand for explanation and articulation.

The opening scene is a prototypical picture of Juliette Fontaine: she is alone in the airport in Nancy, France. She is not just sitting by herself; she is profoundly, existentially isolated, a million miles away from even the people seated just a few feet away. She looks tired, haggard, gaunt, her expressionless eyes receding into dark shadows. Also prototypical: she is here waiting alone because her family seems to have forgotten to pick her up.

27. By that I only mean that the film is very much character driven, a series of psychological studies that is almost "novelistic" in its vignettes and visual meditations. Viewers used to frenetic "entertainment" will be disappointed. One needs to watch *I've Loved You So Long* the way one reads a literary novel.

Eventually Léa, her younger sister, arrives and finds Juliette. Their first encounter in over fifteen years is entirely wordless.[28] The isolation and distance are impressed upon us by the absence of conversation. Finally, in the Volvo on the way home, Léa simply says, "I'm glad you're here."

We are quickly able to piece together Juliette's story: she has been in prison in England for the past fifteen years. She has been physically isolated, rent from the fabric of family and friendship and community. So the very fact that Léa and Luc welcome her into their home is already an undoing of that; she is welcomed, enfolded. Juliette's parole officer emphasizes the point: "Family is important. Solitude isn't good. Man isn't made to be alone." This is from a man who confesses to his own loneliness and isolation. It is clear that he is envious of Juliette; and while he is garrulous, she is largely mute.

But Juliette's reentry is not simple: moments of gratitude are interspersed with waves of resistance, even anger. The welcome of her family and their friends can't undo the existential loneliness that besets her. There is something that will not allow her to connect. And it is clear that Luc is not entirely comfortable with Juliette in the house. He is especially resistant to leaving her alone with their children. Indeed, her past hangs over the entire family as a question waiting to be asked, a mystery that cannot be broached. Luc presses Léa to find out *why*. They are clamoring for an *explanation*. They are asking for *reasons*. Juliette will not be fully welcomed until she enters this space of reasons, this discursive community in which we ask for (and give) reasons. Until then, she will not be fully part of this "we"; she is not one of "us."

As Juliette is inching her way back into civilization, the picture begins to be filled in. When she learns that Léa and Luc adopted both of their children, though both were able to conceive, Juliette remarks plaintively, "Because of me. Because of what I did." We are left puzzled, but with intimations.

Juliette begins looking for work, and her social worker finally lands her a job interview—no mean feat for someone with her record. But it is in the interview that the full horror is disclosed. The gruff, no-nonsense foreman is perusing her resume (and

28. The play on these themes is rife: Léa's husband, Luc, is a lexicographer, but Luc's father, who lives with them, is mute because of a stroke.

record). "Fifteen years?!," he asks with surprise. "Who did you kill?"

Juliette at first hesitates, but then finally *says* it—says *it* quite matter-of-factly: "My son. My six-year-old son."

The foreman is horrified. "Get out," he says in a stupefied whisper. And then in a shout: "Get out!" She is not at all shocked. He simply sees the monster that Juliette has to look at every day in the mirror.

All of those earlier questions about *why* take on a new urgency now. We are just as puzzled as Léa and Luc. *Why* would Juliette do such a thing? And why was she silent during the entire trial? Why has she never *explained* herself?

And yet the community that surrounds her begins to expand. The circle that included Léa, Luc, their children, and Papa swells to include others: friends, coworkers, even the steady presence of her parole officer. We see Juliette almost enjoying herself in the bustle and banter of a dinner party. An excursion to a country house with a wide circle of friends is a day of delight (until it becomes an awkward moment of disclosure). There are moments in which she seems to feel at home in this "we," and she looks back on her isolation with new eyes. One evening she wanders into the library where (mute) Papa reads incessantly. Nestling into the couch, surveying the books strewn about, the oft-silent Juliette confesses to the mute Papa: "In prison I put books by my pillow. Their presence reassured me. A sort of rampart against the world. A world without me. It got along fine without me."

But this last part is not true, and realizing it is the key to Juliette's truly becoming part of this "we," this discursive community. Before she can feel the normative force of the demand for *reasons*—her responsibility to answer the question *why?*—she will have to be enfolded into this community of practice and *feel* that she belongs. She will need to belong before she can believe that this is true. Then, and only then, will the expectations of the community be felt as a demand to which she is willing to submit. And this will not be abstract. It will be as simple as Léa asking, "Why?"

But first Juliette will need her perception challenged and corrected by her immersion in this community. In some ways, this simply requires *remembering* that she belonged. Her conversations with Léa often trek down the road of memory, which is its own kind of know-how, its own implicit understanding shared between two sisters. This is encapsulated when they sit down together at the piano in the attic and play a duet they used to play as girls—they play it effortlessly, "like it was yesterday," and sing together the lyric, "I've loved you so long."

Juliette will continue to struggle to believe this, to *believe* that she belongs, to *know* that she is one of "us." "You forgot me," she charges one day. Léa, hurt, invites her to open a battered cardboard box filled with old diaries and calendars. On each and every page is evidence that pushes back on Juliette's claims: at the beginning of each and every day, Léa had written the name "Juliette" and the number of days she had been away. The world did *not* get along fine without Juliette. In Brandomian terms, we might say that Léa refuses to "license" Juliette's claim, and there are material conditions that contest her version of the story.

At the level of practice, we might say, Juliette is being enfolded into a social body. The isolation of her imprisonment—an isolation, we'll learn, that also *preceded* her imprisonment—is being eroded in all kinds of ways. The intimacy with her sister's family is deepening; her romantic relationship with a fellow named Michel is blossoming; even her place at work is being normalized. When she makes it through a probationary phase and is awarded a permanent contract, the entire community celebrates with her by throwing a party. After the festivities, Juliette simply replies, "Merci." The simplicity of the word is testament to a profound sense of gratitude.

But there remains a distance, a disconnect, a way in which Juliette is absent even when she is present. Indeed, she confesses to Michel that in prison she would always pace in the courtyard by herself. The other women called her "the absent one" (also the name of a character in a Giono novel, Michel points out). That's it: somehow Juliette remains absent. And this is because something still needs to be said. In some way, Juliette will not have entered the community until she also enters the space of reasons in which those around her can ask, "Why did you do that?" And she will have become a full-fledged member of this discursive community when she answers that question, when she *explains* herself, when she gives the reasons that are asked of her.

Or, to look at it from the other side: not until the rest of her community can *make sense* of what she's done will Juliette be one of them. There are things that need to be made explicit in order for the community around her to grapple with the significance of her actions. But Juliette isn't saying anything.

Other aspects of the world impress themselves upon this community of practice; the environment constrains them; things get up to their "antics." One morning, in hastily tidying her room, Juliette jostles a book and, unbeknownst to her, a picture of her dead son, Pierre, falls on the ground, along with a note. When, later that day, one of Léa's daughters brings Léa the photograph, the visage of Pierre comes as a shock, almost a terror. When she returns to Juliette's room, she finds the note: it is a poem by Pierre, scribbled in crayon, penned to his Mama, Juliette, pledging his undying love. The poem is jotted on a scrap of paper from a medical laboratory reporting test results that Léa can't understand. When a friend who is a physician explains the diagnosis, a part of the story that had remained implicit is now made explicit: Pierre was dying a horrible kind of death. Without "justifying" Juliette's actions in an ethical sense, this "making explicit" nonetheless begins to explain—begins to answer *why*—whereas Juliette had always remained silent.

Léa confronts Juliette with this information, broaching the question once again, "Why?" The *why* has a different frame now, a different angle. "We were there," Léa pleads. "Didn't we matter?"

"Do you think others matter then?" Juliette screams. "That one cares what they think or do?"

Again, Léa persists with the question that will enfold Juliette: "Why didn't you tell us? Why? I was there. We were there. We could have helped you."

"Helped me in what way?" scoffs Juliette. It is clear that her existential isolation was in place long before her imprisonment—that, in some way, it was this isolation and loneliness that was a factor in the act that led to her imprisonment. And so even now she can't imagine how others could help. "Helped me in *what* way? What could you have done? When he screamed out in pain, when his limbs started writhing, and when he was choking to death, what could you have done?"

But there is no undoing the past, so Léa emphasizes the present reality: "I'm here. I love you, do you understand? I love you." And it is that *love* that makes her plead with Juliette: "Tell me. Tell me! Go on. Tell me. Say it. Say it!"

This time Juliette will answer the call, will answer the question that is actually inviting her to fully enter into the community, into the space of reasons in which "we" make things explicit. She recounts the beautiful tragedy of her final night with Pierre: the songs and stories followed by the injection and the stillness. When she awoke, "Nothing mattered anymore. I wanted to go to prison. Either way, I was guilty. I'd given birth to him and condemned him to die. And I had nothing to say."

She thinks back to the trial, to all of the questions, to the sort of questions that have been hovering unsaid here in her sister's home. "Explain," she mutters to no one in particular. "Explain what? To whom? Explaining is looking for excuses. Death has no excuses. The worst prison is the death of one's child. You never get out of it."

But once again, what Juliette says does not seem to be true. Because explaining—making explicit—*does* do something. It has done something in this very episode. By explaining, expressing, making explicit what had until now been merely implicit, Juliette is understood, welcomed, even forgiven.

As Léa embraces Juliette, she notices rain dancing on the leaded glass like an abstract painting. She whispers to Juliette, "Look, it's so beautiful." And Juliette is able to smile in agreement.

A door closes below. A voice calls out. It is Michel. "Anyone home?" he calls. "Juliette?"

She hesitates. But then this formerly "absent one"—this one who had been distanced by silence, this one who has finally explained herself and thus been welcomed into the linguistic community—this one answers. "Oui!" she shouts down the stairs. "Je suis la!" And then more quietly to Léa: "Je suis la."

"I am here."

Inferring Reference: Truth and the Social Nature of Objectivity

Let's appreciate the force of Brandom's (somewhat scandalous) proposal: according to his inferentialism, we are "justified" in believing what our friends will let us get away with saying. In other words, we are entitled to those claims that are accepted as good material inferences within a community of practice. What counts as "rational," then, *depends* on the rules and norms of a discursive community. Concepts are *relative to* a community of practice. And

while Brandom has consistently emphasized the *normativity*—
and hence accountability—built into this inferentialist account of
meaning, it is hard for us to shake the nagging sense that this just
allows us to hole up within some "community of practice" where
we can say *whatever we want*. In other words, it still feels like the
dependence-claim (that justification is *relative to* a community of
practice) amounts to arbitrariness, because if inference rather than
reference is the locus of rationality, then it seems like there is no
"reality" to which we are accountable. It feels like we just get to
make up "our own" truth. It might seem that inferentialism leaves
us with the worst sort of sophomoric relativism.

Brandom understands this worry and tries to address it head-on
in the closing chapters of *Articulating Reasons* by articulating a
specifically inferentialist account of truth.

> Besides thinking of sapience in terms of reasons and inference,
> it is natural to think of it in terms of truth. Sapients are believ-
> ers, and believing is taking-true. Sapients are agents, and acting is
> making-true. To be sapient is to have states such as belief, desire,
> and intention, which are contentful in the sense that the question
> can be appropriately raised under what circumstances what is be-
> lieved, desired, or intended would be *true*. Understanding such a
> content is grasping the conditions that are necessary and sufficient
> for its truth. (*AR*, 158)

Our conceptual claims, even if they are governed by inferential
norms, nonetheless have *content*: they are *about* something. And
while the rules governing good inference are relative to a community
of discursive practice, such inferences and such communities are
always already embedded in "circumstances" that are another pole
of dependence. What counts as a "true" claim (a good inferential
move) is relative to the implicit rules of a discursive community;
but it is also relative to a situation, a state of affairs *in which* the
community will "let me get away with" saying it. So while "propositional contents stand in inferential relations," at the same time
"they have truth conditions" (158).

But Brandom is not falling back into a representationalist account. Instead he suggests that "the representational dimension
of propositional contents should be understood in terms of their
social articulation" (158). Thus his goal is to articulate "an account
in nonrepresentational terms of what is expressed by the use of

explicitly representational vocabulary" (166). Note the challenge he faces: "representational vocabulary" is our "folk" vocabulary; the inside/outside picture of representation has effectively seeped down into everyday speech such that most of us, by default, think about our claims in representational terms. Our vocabulary is functionally representationalist. But for all of the reasons that Wittgenstein and Rorty have articulated, Brandom rejects the representationalist paradigm. However, he does not deny the "aboutness" of our claims. So his task is to offer a nonrepresentationalist (i.e., inferentialist) account of "aboutness" that explains the force of our lingering representationalist vocabulary. No mean feat. Here's how it goes.

Kant, you'll recall, taught us that "we" are those creatures who take responsibility for what we say. To be sapient is to be the sorts of creatures who inhabit the "space of reasons," and that space is a *normative* space: it is governed by rules and norms and expectations. In this context, Brandom notes another feature of this Kantian picture: *judgment* is "the fundamental unit of awareness or cognition" because judgments "are the minimal unit one can take *responsibility* for on the cognitive side" (*AR*, 160). Parrots and thermostats can respond and react to environmental conditions, but they don't make *judgments* about them because no one is holding them responsible for their responses. To be a concept user is to be able to make such judgments.[29] And it is our judgments that are characterized by "aboutness."

Our concepts—which make explicit our judgments—are "propositionally contentful" in such a way that they "can serve both as a premise and as the conclusion of *inferences*" (*AR*, 161). When we "take something as true," we license it as something that can be treated as "a fit premise for inferences." We authorize the claim as the basis on which good inferences can be made. Indeed, we might "define truth as what is preserved by good inferences" (161). "Claims both serve as and stand in need of reasons or justifications. They have the contents they have in part in virtue of the role they play in a network of inferences" (162).[30] Knowers—that is, sapient concept users—are

---

29. "The concept *concept* is not intelligible apart from the possibility of such application in *judging*" (*AR*, 160).

30. The qualifier "in part" should not go unnoticed.

able to *use* the differentially elicited response in *inference*. The knower has the practical know-how to situate that response in a network of inferential relations—to tell what follows from something being red or cold, what would be evidence for it, what would be incompatible with it, and so on. For the knower, taking something to be red or cold is making a move in the game of giving and asking for reasons—a move that can justify other moves, be justified by still other moves, and that closes off or precludes still further moves. The parrot and the thermostat lack the concepts in spite of their mastery of the corresponding noninferential differential responsive dispositions, precisely because they lack the practical mastery of the inferential articulation in which grasp of conceptual content consists. (*AR*, 162)

The parrot and thermostat might be able to functionally respond, "It's hot in here." But they cannot know that this is consistent with offering to turn on the air conditioning or open the window, or that the statement is incompatible with offering someone a sweater. That's because "It's hot in here" has no conceptual content for them—it has no "aboutness" and no inferential force because they are not the sorts of creatures who inhabit the "space of reasons." For them, it is not a claim that is situated in a wider web of inferences and implications.

This highlights the fulcrum of Brandom's account: propositionalizing is a *social* activity. Yes, claims and judgments are *about* something, but they are also *for* others. While there is a *ref*erential function to our claims and judgments, it is rooted in our being part of a community of *in*ferential practice. "The representational dimension of discourse reflects the fact that conceptual content is not only *inferentially* articulated but also *socially* articulated. The game of giving and asking for reasons is an essentially *social* practice" (*AR*, 163). Indeed, it seems to me that conceptual content is inferentially articulated *because* it is socially articulated: representation, we might say, is always representation *for* . . . (If a claim is made in private, and no one is there to hear it . . . ?)

Judging, claiming, and propositionalizing are "doings"; in that sense, they are *practices* like other practices. But they are "distinguished from other doings by the kind of *commitment* they involve. Judging or claiming is staking a claim—undertaking a commitment. The conceptual articulation of these commitments, their status as distinctively *discursive* commitments, consists in the way they are liable to demands for *justification*" (*AR*, 164). So linguistic practices—conceptual practices—are "doings" that only "we" undertake. To play the conceptual game is to "get" the rules of inference, and those rules are inherited and absorbed from a community of practice. "Understanding or grasping such a propositional content is a kind of know-how—practical mastery of the game of giving and asking for reasons, being able to tell what is a reason for what, distinguish good reasons from bad" (165). On the one hand, we master this as a kind of know-how: to be able to have a conversation is to know how to keep score, to implicitly understand what counts as a move, what would be a good response, and when one can demand reasons, and so on. If we are encountered by a state of affairs in which I'm disposed to say, "That is a red ball," but you say, "That is a green ball," then I'm going to question whether you are *entitled* to that claim. Is that a *commitment* you want to make? Are you willing to take *responsibility* for that proposition? Are you willing to sign up for the implications of saying it's green? Because "in making an as-sertion one also undertakes a *responsibility*—to justify the claim if appropriately challenged" (165). On the other hand, we can also *express* this implicit know-how, *make explicit* the rules of inference that govern our discursive practice. Such articulation is the work of logic.

Justification, on this model, is a social practice: "the intraper-sonal, intercontent inheritance of entitlement to commitments" (*AR*, 165). My claims are *about* things, but they are made within the *social* "space of reasons" and discursive practice. While my claims are responsive to—and made within—environmental con-ditions, it is the discursive community that accepts, endorses, and authorizes "good" inferences. The "assessment of what people are talking and thinking *about*, rather than what they are saying about it, is a feature of the essentially *social* context of *communi-cation*. Talk about representation is talk about what it is to secure communication by being able to use one another's judgments as reasons, as premises in our own inferences" (167–68). Your claims will "score" *as* representations just to the extent that others ("we") are able to take them up and successfully employ them as premises in further inferences. What you *give* as a reason I can *take* as one and *take up* as a premise in other successful inferences; then your claim is *true*. When you are unable to give such reasons, or when your reasons don't accord with the environmental conditions that we share—when your claims don't seem to be "about" the state of affairs in front of us—then your claim is not going to be justified or authorized. If discursive practice is a kind of "score keeping," as Brandom often puts it, then it is important to remember that one can *lose*. That's what it is to be wrong: to not be awarded a point, to not make a good inferential move. In this way, we might say that "representation" is something that is *conferred* by a community of discursive practice.

One can get a sense of how Brandom thus accounts for "objectivity." Instead of rooting objectivity in some magical "correspondence" between inside and outside, the picture is one of a certain kind of "convertability": those claims are "objective" that can be taken up and successfully employed by others in good inferences. "The social dimension of inference involved in the communication to others of claims that must be available as reasons both to the speaker and to the audience, in spite of differences in collateral commitments, is what underlies the representational dimension of discourse" (*AR*, 183).

In the final chapter of *Articulating Reasons*, Brandom addresses this more directly. Assertions, he recognizes, "are subject to two essential but fundamentally differently kinds of normative appraisal": (1) "We can ask whether an assertion is correct in the sense that the speaker was entitled to make it"; and (2) "we can also ask whether the assertion is correct in the sense of being *true*, in the sense that things are as it claims they are" (*AR*, 187). In the first sense, we're asking whether the concept user is following the rules—a matter of entitlement, authorization, and justification. In the second sense, we are questioning the "aboutness" of the claim.

Brandom's project is to secure an account of objectivity without lapsing back into the representationalism that is assumed behind realist, "correspondence" accounts of objectivity. His goal is to explain how propositional contents can be "objective *in the sense of* swinging free of the attitudes of the linguistic practitioners who deploy them in assertions" (*AR*, 188, emphasis added). A claim will be "objective" in this sense if it is not idiosyncratically tethered to subjective impressions; that is, an "objective" claim is one that can be *shared* because it doesn't depend on the attitudes of specific linguistic practitioners. However, that doesn't mean that it doesn't *depend* on other factors and conditions. To say that an "objective" claim swings free of the attitudes of linguistic practitioners is not the same as saying it is free of all conditions or independent of the community of discursive practice. Brandom has belabored the point that all claims are always and only made within the "space of reasons" that is forged in a linguistic community. Thus he's after "*objectivity* of a particular sort" (190).

Objective propositions, then, are subject to the two sorts of *normative* evaluation we noted above: Do they follow the rules of inference? And are they true? On the first normative issue, the question is whether a statement or proposition "counts" *as* an assertion—whether it counts as a move in a game of giving and asking for reasons (*AR*, 189). In this respect, a performance counts as an assertion if it involves *commitment* and *entitlement*. To count as an assertion "a move must not be idle, it must make a difference, it must have consequences for what else it is appropriate to do, according to the rules of the game" (191). The responses of parrots and thermostats are "idle" just because they don't take responsibility for them—which is why they are not subject to *normative* evaluation. So, ironically, the sort of environmental detection carried out by a thermostat does not count as "objectivity" for Brandom because there is no element of normativity involved. Only "we" can make objective claims because making a claim is "taking up a particular sort of normative stance toward an inferentially articulated content. It is *endorsing* it, taking *responsibility* for it, *committing* oneself to it" (192). This is why we are liable to demands for justification (193).

But it is the second element of normativity that is closer to the usual terrain of objectivity. For Brandom, "contents display *objectivity* of a particular sort" when "they are not about any constellation of attitudes on the part of the linguistic practitioners who produce and consume them as reasons" (*AR*, 190). His concern is that our judgments not be merely "subjective." In fact, these two aspects of normativity interact: the community of discursive practice will grant entitlement to claims that are compatible *under the right conditions*. Or, to state it negatively, "two assertible contents are *incompatible* in case *commitment* to one precludes *entitlement* to the other" (194). Incompatibility is a kind of case study in Brandom's inferentialist account of objectivity. For example, "Commitment to the content expressed by the sentence 'The swatch is red' rules out entitlement to the commitment that would

be undertaken by asserting the sentence 'The swatch is green'"
(194). There is a twofold constraint on our games/moves here: On
the one hand, it is a matter of what the discursive community will
"license"—what your peers will let you get away with. On the other
hand, your peers in the discursive community are constrained by
environmental conditions, by "the circumstances" and states of
affairs that constrain whether or not it is a good *material* inference
given the matter of swatches and redness we bump up against. So
the "objectivity" of my claim *depends on* the discursive community, but it also seems to *depend on* something like environmental
conditions and material facts—what Brandom simply describes
as "circumstances" (200). Your peers are going to let you get away
with calling the swatch red in those circumstances where it is agreed
that this sort of material is successfully described as red.

However, before your realist heart gets too warmed and you
feel like you've just caught Brandom backsliding into representation and correspondence, listen carefully to his account of this
"circumstantial" constraint.

> The point of all this is that the *objectivity* of propositional con-
> tent—the fact that in claiming that the swatch is red we are not
> saying anything about who could appropriately assert anything,
> or about who is committed or entitled to what, *are indeed saying
> something that could be true even if there had never been rational
> beings*—is a feature we can make intelligible as a structure of the
> commitments and entitlements that articulate the *use* of sentences.
> (*AR*, 203, emphases added)

As in Wittgenstein, reference is a kind of *use*; representation
is a game we can play, and a game that gets all kinds of "work"
done—not because the words magically hook onto (exterior)
things but because the discursive community successfully *copes*
with the world when we deal with *these* circumstances with claims
about red swatches, and so on. The incompatibilities are generated *by* the social (linguistic) practices: "*All* that is required is that
the commitments and entitlements *linguistic practices associate
with* ordinary empirical claims such as 'The swatch is red' generate incompatibilities" (*AR*, 203, latter emphasis added). The
incompatibility is generated *within the space of reasons*, though
in response to environmental conditions and material factors.

"Objectivity" does not lift us up out of our contingency, creature-hood, and community.

What Brandom offers in this model are resources to appreciate the contingency and dependence of knowledge and truth without lapsing into "fideism" or some kind of epistemic tribalism that leaves us unaccountable to those who disagree. This has significant implications for how we think about Christian proclamation and apologetics, to which we now turn in the final chapter.

5

The (Inferential) Nature of Doctrine

Postliberalism as Christian Pragmatism

How might Brandom's inferentialism, his "rationalist" pragmatism, help us understand Christian theology and doctrine?[1] And how might his account of the relationship between implicit know-*how* and explicit (articulated) know-*that* provide a framework to understand the relationship between worship and theology, between religious practice and doctrinal articulation?

1. By now it should be clear that I am primarily interested in pragmatism as an account of *meaning*, and specifically meaning *as* "use." This is why I have focused on a pragmatist thread that runs from Wittgenstein through Rorty up to Brandom, rather than the pragmatism of John Dewey and William James. The latter's "pragmatism," if I can (over)simplify it, is more concerned with practice *and its effects* or consequences as a criterion for truth. "You shall know them by their *fruits*" is the mantra of this line of pragmatist thought—and this too is a pragmatist theme in Rorty. My focus on a pragmatist account of meaning does not preclude this other emphasis; it's just that it doesn't fall within the purview of my interest in philosophy of language. For a "Christian pragmatism" that takes up this latter stream, see the work of Cornel West, including *The American Evasion of Philosophy: A Geneaology of Pragmatism* (Madison: University of Wisconsin Press, 1989); and "On Prophetic Pragmatism," in *The Cornel West Reader* (New York: Basic Books, 1999), 149–73.

In some ways, these questions were already answered in 1984, ten years before Brandom published *Making It Explicit*. Indebted to Wittgenstein, George Lindbeck's landmark book *The Nature of Doctrine* sketched a "cultural-linguistic" or "postliberal" understanding of religion and doctrine that is fundamentally *pragmatist* in its account of theological meaning while at the same time fundamentally *missional* in its understanding of the church's task of proclamation in a post-Christian culture.[2] While Lindbeck is concerned with the nature of *doctrine*, his project requires a fundamental reconsideration of *religion*, of the priority of lived religious *practice* as the soil from which doctrine grows. He offers a theoretical account that argues that Christian faith is *not* primarily theoretical but is better understood as a kind of know-*how*.

To grasp Lindbeck's proposal is to get a feel for the lineaments of a Christian pragmatism. So you might think of *Who's Afraid of Relativism?* as the long-lost prequel to Lindbeck's book. Or perhaps better: my engagement with pragmatism could be seen as a more explicitly philosophical path to a similar account of the relationship between practice and theory, worship and doctrine, ultimately prompting us to think of Christianity primarily as a "form of life" rather than an intellectual system.[3] At the same time, I hope this philosophical engagement with pragmatism will provide the theoretical back story for Lindbeck's influential proposal, perhaps serving to deflect and deflate certain criticisms. Indeed, trying to read Lindbeck without understanding Wittgenstein is like trying to read Derrida without understanding Husserl, or trying to read John Calvin without knowing anything of St. Augustine.[4] So I hope this brief primer on pragmatism can be received as the philosophical springboard for understanding postliberalism, which is, in many ways, an embodiment of the religious and theological implications of pragmatism.

---

2. George Lindbeck, *The Nature of Doctrine: Religion and Theology in a Postliberal Age* (Philadelphia: Westminster, 1984); henceforth abbreviated in the text as *ND*. He notes that his approach "could also be called 'postmodern'" (135n1).

3. This is why I also see *Who's Afraid of Relativism?* as providing the philosophical framework to account for the relationship between worship and doctrine that I sketch out in my Cultural Liturgies project (*Desiring the Kingdom*; *Imagining the Kingdom*).

4. For example, Kevin Vanhoozer's criticisms of Lindbeck fail to appreciate the pragmatist account of knowledge that is beneath *Nature of Doctrine*.

But what is "postliberalism"? "Postliberalism" has been a term used loosely to describe a number of related developments and schools of thought in contemporary theology, including the "Yale school" of Lindbeck and Hans Frei as well as Paul Holmer[5] and his student Stanley Hauerwas. But it can also encompass other schools of thought like Radical Orthodoxy and some streams that flow from the heritage of Karl Barth.[6] In heuristic terms, what they share in common is a renewed emphasis on the *ecclesial* nature of theology, emphasizing the priority of liturgical *practice* as the source and site for theological articulation. In short, postliberalism returns religion to practice and returns theology to the church. To put this in Wittgensteinian terms, postliberalism emphasizes that Christianity is a "form of life" found first and foremost in the community of practice that is the church. In other words, Christian faith (and religion more generally) is a kind of know-*how*; theology and doctrine, then, "make explicit" our know-how as know-*that* claims, articulating the norms implicit in the practices of the community that is the body of Christ.

Since Lindbeck's *Nature of Doctrine* was both a crystallization of and catalyst for postliberalism, and since he explicitly draws on Wittgenstein (and Wittgensteinian social scientists like Clifford Geertz and Peter Winch), I will conclude by unpacking the key aspects of Lindbeck's postliberal vision. In doing so, I hope we'll at once see the implications of a Christian pragmatism *and* retroactively frame the pragmatist tradition as the philosophical wells from which Lindbeck's proposal drinks.

5. On Holmer, see D. Stephen Long, *Speaking of God: Theology, Language, and Truth* (Grand Rapids: Eerdmans, 2009), 220–21; and Lindbeck, *ND*, 28.

6. I provide a "map" of these movements in *Introducing Radical Orthodoxy: Mapping a Post-Secular Theology* (Grand Rapids: Baker Academic, 2004), 25–30. For an excellent introduction from a Roman Catholic perspective but of ecumenical interest, see Robert Barron, *The Priority of Christ: Toward a Postliberal Catholicism* (Grand Rapids: Brazos, 2007). See also the conversations and analysis in John Wright, ed., *Postliberal Theology and the Church Catholic: Conversations with George Lindbeck, David Burrell, and Stanley Hauerwas* (Grand Rapids: Baker Academic, 2012). Lindbeck himself avers to a "second hand" influence of Barth on his project, via the work of his Yale colleagues David Kelsey and above all, Hans Frei (*ND*, 135). For critical discussion, see Paul DeHart, *The Trial of the Witnesses: The Rise and Decline of Postliberal Theology* (Oxford: Blackwell, 2006).

A Theory of Practice: What's the Use of Doctrine?

Lindbeck's quarry is a theory *of* doctrine. As such, he isn't exploring specific doctrine*s* (e.g., How should we understand the two natures of Christ? Or how should we think about the Eucharist?).[7] Instead, he is asking *meta-* questions: What *is* "doctrine"? What is the relationship between doctrine and religious practice? What's the difference between "doctrine" and "theology"? But as soon as we begin to explore the nature of *doctrine*, we are immediately forced to reconsider what we mean by "religion." "Theories of religion and of doctrine are interdependent," Lindbeck notes, "and deficiencies in one area are inseparable from deficiencies in the other." This is why "a postliberal way of conceiving religion and religious doctrine is called for" (*ND*, 7).[8]

The postliberal approach is an alternative to two other dominant ways of thinking about religion and doctrine that Lindbeck describes as the "cognitive-propositional" and "experiential-expressive" models. What distinguishes all of these models, including Lindbeck's, is how they construe the *function* of doctrine—the *use* of doctrine. In the *cognitive-propositional* model, "church doctrines function as informative propositions or truth claims about objective realities" (*ND*, 16). He sees this as a largely *pre*modern approach—"the approach of traditional orthodoxies (as well as of many heterodoxies)"—but also notes this model "has certain affinities to the outlook on religion adopted by much modern Anglo-American analytic philosophy with its preoccupation with the cognitive or informational meaningfulness of religious utterances"

---

7. Though, as Lindbeck constantly emphasizes, the whole point of a postliberal account *of* doctrine is to help us better understand doctrine*s*, and specifically be able to specify the criteria for what would count as "faithful" changes to a doctrinal tradition as well as how we might think about doctrinal (dis)agreement (*ND*, 7, 74–75, 112).

8. It is clear that Lindbeck is primarily concerned with understanding Christianity, but he also believes that the cultural-linguistic model has purchase for understanding other religions; thus, he tends to employ the generic term "religion." My exposition follows him in this, but context will make it clear that our primary concern under the rubric of "religion" is lived Christian faith, even especially the practices of Christian worship. It is important to remember that what Lindbeck calls "religion" is not something abstract but in fact always and only a concrete "form of life" (per Wittgenstein). "The focus is on particular religions rather than on religious universals" (*ND*, 23).

(ND, 16).[9] For reasons we'll see in a moment, he believes this has been largely displaced by the experiential-expressive approach in modernity, but for those who inhabit certain "conservative" sectors of evangelicalism, the cognitive-propositional model will sound very familiar. Of philosophical interest here is that, in order for the cognitive-propositional approach to endure in modernity, it must be wed to (and founded upon) a representationalist account of knowledge—just the picture of knowledge called into question by pragmatism.

But on this score, the *experiential-expressive* approach is equally indebted to what Charles Taylor calls the "inside/outside" (I/O) picture of knowledge and truth. It's just that for experiential-expressive approaches, the direction goes the other way: instead of an "outside" being represented "inside" the mind, doctrine is thought of primarily as the exterior expression of an inward religious experience. Doctrines, then, are merely feeble and fickle "expressions" that attempt to "put into words" an inward religious experience that is universal. This is why experiential-expressive approaches tend to treat doctrines as entirely fungible and revisable; indeed, they can even treat different religions as merely different ways of trying to "express" this inward *human* experience. "There is thus at least the logical possibility [on the experiential-expressive account] that a Buddhist and a Christian might have basically the same faith, although expressed very differently" (ND, 17).[10]

Lindbeck sees the experiential-expressive model as the dominant picture of religion in modernity. Indeed, "the habits of thought it has fostered are ingrained in the soul of the modern West," which has been characterized by "the experiential-expressive turn to the subject" (ND, 21, 24).[11] His assessment of the coming religious landscape, from the perspective of 1984, is prescient: "As

9. I have expanded this evaluation and thesis in "Philosophy of Religion Takes Practice: Liturgy as Source and Method in Philosophy of Religion," in *Contemporary Practice and Method in the Philosophy of Religion: New Essays*, ed. David Cheetham and Rolfe King (London: Continuum, 2008), 133–47.

10. Thus Lindbeck sees the experiential-expressive approach embodied in Schleiermacher's "feeling of absolute dependence" and Tillich's "ground of being"—both taken to be universal religious phenomena that can find different expressions. As he later notes, "Cultural-linguistic theorists [like Lindbeck] are unimpressed by efforts to show that all religions are basically similar" (ND, 41).

11. This historical claim accords with Charles Taylor's account of modernity as the "age of authenticity" (in Taylor, *Sources of the Self* and *A Secular Age*).

we move into a culturally (even if not statistically) post-Christian period . . . increasing numbers of people regard all religions as possible sources of symbols to be used eclectically in articulating, clarifying, and organizing the experiences of the inner self. Religions are seen as multiple suppliers of different forms of a single commodity needed for transcendent self-expression and self-realization" (*ND*, 22). Thus he recognizes the overwhelming "attractiveness" of the experiential-expressive model in modernity, in our age of authenticity in which sincerity of self-expression is the highest good (*ND*, 23).

At this point some of us might be nodding in agreement, thinking that this experiential-expressive approach is precisely what's wrong with "liberal" Christianity. But the net of Lindbeck's point is much wider than that: it catches a lot of "conservative" Christianity as well—namely, all of those forms of Christianity that effectively treat the gospel as an inward, privatized experience between "me and Jesus." There's more than one way to embody the experiential-expressive paradigm, and many versions of evangelicalism *function* in the same way: they begin from an appeal to inner experience and, in the name of "relevance," seek to "adapt" Christianity to different forms that are treated as completely interchangeable. In other words, on Lindbeck's account, all sorts of conservative evangelicals are "liberals"—and not just "emergent"-types.[12] At this juncture, Lindbeck lays out "the crucial difference" between liberals and postliberals: "Liberals start with an experience, with an account of the present, and then adjust their vision of the kingdom of God accordingly, while postliberals are in principle committed to doing the reverse. The first procedure makes it easier to accommodate to present trends, whether from the right or the left: Christian fellow travelers of both Nazism and Stalinism generally

12. In a concluding panel discussion at a conference on evangelicals and postliberalism, hosted by Wheaton College, Lindbeck wryly observed: "I find myself very far to the right, theologically, of most evangelicals. I knew this before, but I became more conscious of it at this conference. I'm much more creedal than most of the people here. I place more emphasis on creeds, confessions and dogmas. I'm sacramentally realistic in a way that free church people are not. I have a much higher ecclesiology than most of the people here. So for me it's not at all a dialogue between the left and the right. It's much more complicated than that." See "A Panel Discussion," in *The Nature of Confession: Evangelicals and Postliberals in Conversation*, ed. Timothy R. Phillips and Dennis L. Okholm (Downers Grove, IL: InterVarsity, 1996), 247.

used liberal methodology to justify their positions" (*ND*, 126). By fixating on an inward experience and functionally excluding essential communal practices from "religion," the experiential-expressive ("liberal") model is all the more easily absorbed by other regnant visions and ideologies, blown about by every wind in the name of "relevance."[13] Again, Lindbeck's anticipation of what was to come seems to have been prophetic.

> Sociologists have been telling us for a hundred years or more that the rationalization, pluralism, and mobility of modern life dissolve the bonds of tradition and community. This produces multitudes of men and women who are impelled, if they have religious yearnings, to embark on their own individual quests for symbols of transcendence. *The churches have become purveyors of this commodity rather than communities that socialize their members into coherent and comprehensive religious outlooks and forms of life.* (*ND*, 126, emphasis added)[14]

We should note that he doesn't qualify the claim and say "liberal" churches are doing this. Anywhere that Christianity is interiorized and de-practiced, we might say, we are on the terrain of experiential-expressive approaches that exhibit this commodification, even if they loudly claim to be "conservative," "Bible-based," and "gospel-centered." In sum, those churches that foster "moralistic therapeutic deism" are purveying experiential-expressive Christianity.[15]

13. This very much parallels Ross Douthat's account of American Christianity's assimilation to American culture, hinging on the fact that American Christianity effectively deinstitutionalized Christian faith, "privatizing" it as an inner experience. See Ross Douthat, *Bad Religion: How We Became a Nation of Heretics* (New York: Free Press, 2012), 139–41, 273.

14. He continues: "Society paradoxically conditions human beings to experience selfhood as somehow prior to social influences, and Eastern religions and philosophies are utilized to support what, from a cultural-linguistic perspective, is the myth of the transcendental ego. Selfhood is experienced as a given rather than as either a gift or an achievement, and fulfillment comes from exfoliating or penetrating into the inner depths rather than from communally responsible action in the public world" (*ND*, 126).

15. "Moralistic therapeutic deism" is Christian Smith's term to describe the functionally heterodox view of God that seems to be absorbed by most young people in the United States, including those fostered in "evangelical" contexts. See Christian Smith, with Melinda Lundquist Denton, *Soul Searching: The Religious and Spiritual Lives of American Teenagers* (New York: Oxford University Press, 2005), 118–70.

Lindbeck sees weaknesses in both of these models, in terms of both their inability to account for the "phenomenon" of religious practice and their inability to make sense of doctrinal development and change. Practically, Lindbeck is concerned that these other models—particularly the experiential-expressive—deemphasize (yea, *gut*) the practices of religious communities, which does not bode well for the future of Christianity. While the experiential-expressive is the dominant model in modernity, Lindbeck seems to suggest that even the cognitive-propositional model that endures is changed in its modern context, absorbing the same I/O picture of knowledge. Furthermore, the cognitive-propositional model mirrors the experiential-expressive model by similarly deemphasizing religious *practices*, treating religion as primarily a set of informational propositions. So both of these models fail to appreciate religion (Christianity) as a "form of life" in the Wittgensteinian sense. We can add a further reason to reject these other models: in light of the critiques of Wittgenstein, Rorty, and Brandom, we would also note that both of these models are rooted in a problematic epistemology that is committed to the I/O picture. They are both dependent upon a representationalist account of meaning that pragmatism has discredited. So the constructive task of *Nature of Doctrine* is to outline a very different model, a "cultural-linguistic" approach that circumvents this epistemological trap while also revaluing the significance of religious practice as essential and central to "religion" (in this case, Christianity).

Echoing developments in anthropology and philosophy, the *cultural-linguistic* model considers religion less an intellectual "system" or personal "expression" and more akin to "languages together with their correlative forms of life"—as "idioms for the construing of reality and the living of life" (*ND*, 18).[16] So religion

16. In a way, Lindbeck's method in *The Nature of Doctrine* mirrors what he claims about religion and theology. As he confesses at the beginning, "The case developed in this book . . . is circular rather than linear. Its persuasiveness, if any, does not depend on moving step by step in a demonstrative sequence, but on the illuminating power of the whole. It may be that if light dawns, it will be over the whole landscape simultaneously" (11). (In support, he cites Wittgenstein, *On Certainty*, ed. G. E. M. Anscombe and G. H. von Wright [Oxford: Blackwell, 1969], §105: "All testing, all confirmation and disconfirmation of a hypothesis takes place already within a system. And this system is not a more or less arbitrary and doubtful point of departure for all our arguments: no, it belongs to the essence of what we call an argument. The system is not so much the point of departure, as the element in which arguments have their

is more like learning how to be a member of the tribe, how to be a citizen of your country, how to speak your first language. Religion (e.g., Christianity) is not a set of propositions that one believes but rather a (communal) way of life. Religion will be a matter more of initiation than of information, a matter of know-*how* before it ever becomes a matter of know-*that*. In the cultural-linguistic model, "religions are seen as comprehensive interpretive schemes, usually embodied in myths or narratives and heavily ritualized, which structure human experience and understanding of self and world" (*ND*, 32). Contrary to the cognitive-propositional model, religion is "not primarily an array of beliefs" but more like a "set of skills" (33). But contrary to the individualism and subjectivism of the experiential-expressive approach, the cultural-linguistic model emphasizes the essentially *communal* character of religion: "Like a culture or language, it is a communal phenomenon that shapes the subjectivities of individuals rather than being primarily a manifestation of those subjectivities" (33).

One could starkly—if a bit simplistically—get a sense for the radical difference between the experiential-expressive and the cultural-linguistic by saying that the cultural-linguistic approach "reverses the relation of the inner and the outer. Instead of deriving external features of religion from inner experience, it is the inner experiences which are viewed as derivative" (*ND*, 34). Discipleship, then, is a kind of acculturation: "To become religious involves becoming skilled in the language, the symbol system of a given religion. To become a Christian involves learning the story of Israel and of Jesus well enough to interpret and experience oneself and one's world in its terms" (34). In short, a religion is essentially bound up with the communal *form* of its practices (35): the material practices precede and shape the subjectivity of adherents, making it possible to experience and construe the world in certain ways. It takes a village to have an "experience."

---

life.") In language we have used above to describe Wittgenstein and Rorty, we could simply describe this as Lindbeck's *holism*. In a way, one needs to "try on" a whole new "picture"—be inculcated into a new (theoretical) practice—in order to be able to see the whole anew. And the only "proof" or demonstration that is possible, then, is the power of the new picture to help one make sense of the whole, and to feel its superiority to one's prior account. As we'll see momentarily, Lindbeck says religions function in the same way, which has important implications for how we think about apologetics.

This is also why Lindbeck thinks a cultural-linguistic approach is going to face an uphill battle in modernity: it says that religion is only a religion if it impinges upon that most cherished achievement of modernity—our autonomy. "The modern mood is antipathetic to the very notion of communal norms" (*ND*, 77). A model of religion that emphasizes "interiorizing outlooks that others have created, and mastering skills that others have honed" runs counter to the independence, autonomy, and "do-it-yourself-ness" that is affirmed in the experiential-expressive model. "The mere idea that becoming religious might on occasion be rather like achieving competence in the totally non-optional grammatical patterns and lexical resources of a foreign tongue seems alienating and oppressive, an infringement of freedom and choice, a denial of creativity, and repugnant to all the most cherished values of modernity" (*ND*, 22).[17] The cultural-linguistic model, precisely because it hearkens back to *pre*modern religion, is not bound to be popular in our subjectivist age of authenticity.

Lindbeck's is a "cultural" model of religion because it emphasizes these dynamics of formation, socialization, and acculturation—all of which happen on the (implicit) level of know-*how*. The model is "linguistic" because this is how we learn a first language: it is caught, not taught. "To become religious—no less than to become culturally or linguistically competent—is to interiorize a set of skills by practice and training. One learns how to feel, act, and think in conformity with a religious tradition that is, in its inner structure, far richer and more subtle than can be explicitly articulated" (*ND*, 35). A religion works like a language in this respect: "It comprises a vocabulary of discursive and nondiscursive symbols together with a distinctive logic or grammar in terms of which this vocabulary can be meaningfully deployed" (33). Note that final emphasis: this is a language to be *used*, put to work in a way of life. So, as Lindbeck notes, it's more like what Wittgenstein called a "language-game" that is correlated with a "form of life" (33). Now, as a "form of life," a religion has "both cognitive and behavioral dimensions" (33). But in the postliberal approach, as with Brandom, our *doings* precede our *thinkings*. Practice is primary.

17. He goes on to note that "this is true even among theological conservatives, as is illustrated by the stress placed on conversion experiences by the heirs of pietism and revivalism" (*ND*, 22).

> A comprehensive scheme or story used to structure all dimensions
> of existence is not primarily a set of propositions to be believed,
> but is rather the medium in which one moves, a set of skills that
> one employs in living one's life. Its vocabulary of symbols and its
> syntax may be used for many purposes, only one of which is the
> formulation of statements about reality. Thus while a religion's
> truth claims are often of the utmost importance to it (as in the case
> of Christianity), it is, nevertheless, the conceptual vocabulary and
> the syntax or inner logic which determine the kinds of truth claims
> the religion can make. The cognitive aspect, while often important,
> is not primary. (ND, 35)[18]

It should be noted up front that Lindbeck's cultural-linguistic
model does not preclude propositional claims or cognitive dimensions of Christian faith. However, as with pragmatism, Lindbeck
recontextualizes—and de-prioritizes—the cognitive-propositional
aspect; and yet in doing so, he will also be able to provide an account of reference and propositional claims that is similar to that
offered by Rorty and Brandom. We will return to this below.

Saying *That* We Know *How*: A "Rule" Theory of Doctrine

"Religion," on the cultural-linguistic account, is the know-*how* of
a people that makes it possible for me to know-*that*. A religious
community is an instance of just the sort of community of practice described by Wittgenstein, Rorty, and Brandom: a community
engaged in a project, that provides the context for meaning, and
that "trains" me how to "use" the world in certain ways that are
relative to the project/*telos*/identity of the community. In Brandomian terms, we might say that religion is first and foremost on the
plane of the "implicit."

But let's recall that Lindbeck's task is to understand the nature
of *doctrine*. He revisits the nature of religion (emphasizing religious *practice*) in order to discern the nature of doctrine. So where
exactly does doctrine fit in this picture? On the cultural-linguistic
model, the *nature* of doctrine is determined by its *function*. To
answer the question, "What *is* doctrine?" we need to answer the

---

18. Lindbeck's use of the word "cognitive" in this context is not precise. He seems
to use the word as roughly synonymous with "propositional."

question, "What does doctrine *do*?" What function does it play within the community of practice that is a religious community (like the church)? Now, in fact, all three models are distinguished by how doctrine functions: in the cognitive-propositional, doctrines are primarily used to make truth claims; in the experiential-expressive, doctrines are used to express interior feelings and experiences. "The function of church doctrines that becomes most prominent" in the cultural-linguistic model "is their use, not as expressive symbols or as truth claims, but as communally authoritative rules of discourse, attitude, and action." Thus Lindbeck calls this a "regulative" or "rule" theory of doctrine. When religion is understood to be a kind of "culture," an *ethos*, a form of life that enables us to live life, then doctrine functions as the articulated rules that govern our communal life. Lindbeck emphasizes that this "rule" account of doctrine is by no means novel. "The notion of *regulae fidei* goes back to the earliest Christian centuries, and later historians and systematic theologians have often recognized in varying degrees that the operational logic of religious teaching in their communally authoritative (or, as we shall simply say, doctrinal) role is regulative." This is just to recognize that "the task of doctrines is to recommend and exclude certain ranges of—among other things—propositional utterances and symbolizing activities" (*ND*, 18–19). The cultural-linguistic model can be thought of as a robust way to understand the dynamic relationship between *lex orandi* and *lex credendi*—the rule of prayer *as* the rule of belief.

Embedded in the regulative theory of doctrine is not just an account of its function, but also an account of the relationship between doctrine and practice, between theology and worship. If doctrines function as "rules" for the community of (religious) practice, this is only because those doctrines make explicit the norms that were already embedded in the community's practice. In other words, doctrines make explicit the know-how that was already implicit in our practice. To confess that Jesus is "God from God, Light from Light, true God from true God" is to *articulate* what was already implicit in our prayers, a worshipful way of life nourished by the Scriptures. So doctrine is "expressive" in *Brandom*'s sense of the word. Here we need to immediately clear up a possible confusion. Given that Brandom often describes his model as "expressivist," we might be tempted to think that his pragmatist account accords with the experiential-expressive model that

Lindbeck rejects. But that is not the case. As Brandom emphasizes, his expressivism is not a Romantic notion of an "inside" making its way "outside." Nor is his expressivism focused on individual self-expression. To the contrary, Brandom invites us to understand "the process of expression . . . as a matter *not* of transforming what is inner into what is outer but of making *explicit* what is *implicit*" (*AR*, 8). So Brandom's inferentialism is a *communal* expressivism, not a mode of individual expression; and what gets "expressed" are the norms that govern communal practice: the implicit rules that govern our social practice, of which we have know-*how*, are made explicit, articulated in concepts.

In fact, Brandom's account of *inference* is a helpful supplement to Lindbeck on this score. In particular, Brandom's emphasis on *material* inference is an illuminating framework for understanding how doctrine functions according to Lindbeck. What counts as a good inference—a "good move" in the game—is bound up with the *matter* that is under discussion. The evaluation of whether to affirm the Nicene *homoousios* or the semi-Arian *homoiousios* is not a matter that can be settled by "formal" logic.[19] Which of these is a good move, a good inference, is inextricably bound to the *matter* of the community of practice who are heirs of the apostles' teaching, who receive and read and inhabit the world of Scripture, and who pray to Jesus. That "first order" of prayer and proclamation is on the plane of know-*how*; doctrines as formulated in the Nicene Creed are the fruit of the community of Christian practice "making explicit" the norms that were previously unsaid. Doctrines *say* what, up to that point, we previously *did*, in a sense.

In doing so, the community of practice is able to discern what counts as faithful practice. As Brandom puts it, in a different context,

> The expressive task of making material inferential commitments explicit plays an essential role in the reflectively rational Socratic practice of harmonizing our commitments. For a commitment to become explicit is for it to be thrown into the game of giving and asking for reasons as something whose justification, in terms of other commitments and entitlements, is liable to question. (*AR*, 76)

19. Lindbeck alludes to this issue at *ND*, 76.

This helps articulate what Lindbeck seems to mean by a "rule" theory of doctrine. He regularly describes doctrines as "second order" only because doctrines are, in a sense, *derivative* from practice. Like Brandom's account of logic, which bubbles up as the made-explicit rules implicit in our practice, so doctrines in Lindbeck's model are not primarily claims *about* God or the world; instead, they are rules that govern how we can speak about God and God's relationship to the world on the "first-order" level of prayer and proclamation. Church doctrine is a "guide to the fundamental interconnections within a religion" (*ND*, 81).[20] In other words, doctrines are about the inferential relationship *between* confessional claims and not the *referential* relation between our claims and the world. "Doctrines regulate truth claims by excluding some and permitting others" (*ND*, 19), but they don't manufacture the criteria for such regulation. Instead, they make explicit the norms already implicit in the biblical narrative and, in turn, Christian practice. By making things explicit, Brandom emphasizes, we (i.e., the relevant community of practice) can begin to discern inconsistencies, seek to harmonize our commitments, and, in some cases, renew and redirect our practice accordingly. Christian doctrine can be understood to play the same role: to make explicit the commitments implied in our proclamation, prayer, and praise (all of which themselves "live off of" the narrative world of Scripture that is the self-communication of the Triune God). Thus doctrine

---

20. Thus in his concluding chapter Lindbeck, somewhat unhelpfully, describes the postliberal account as "intratextual" rather than "extratextual" (the latter being the stance shared by both the cognitive-propositional and experiential-expressive approaches [*ND*, 114]). The point is that for postliberals, "the meaning is immanent. Meaning is constituted by the uses of a specific language rather than being distinguishable from it. Thus the proper way to determine what 'God' signifies, for example, is by examining how the word operates within a religion and thereby shapes reality and experience" (114). The intention is a good one: nothing less than to emphasize that "the text . . . absorbs the world, rather than the world the text" (118)—that in fact it is the unique primacy of the religious vision that shapes our understanding of the world. However, the language of "intratextual" has led to misunderstandings, as if Lindbeck is insulating religious claims from any "responsibility" to extratextual reality, thereby extolling some kind of linguistic/biblicistic idealism. One can see that Lindbeck does not intend this when he claims, for instance, that understanding scriptural texts "intratextually" is "a matter of explicating their contexts *and the perspectives on extratextual reality that they generate*" (*ND*, 117, emphasis added).

articulates the norms implicit in our practice. Doctrines function as the rules of the Christian language-game.[21]

It's not surprising, then, that Lindbeck, picking up on a hint from Wittgenstein, suggests we think of theology as the *grammar* of the religious/linguistic community of practice.[22] If religion is like a language, which is primarily *used* (spoken, written) to get things *done*, then doctrine is to the community of religious practice as grammar is to a community of linguistic practice. "Just as grammar by itself affirms nothing either true or false regarding the world in which language is used"—since grammar governs how one uses the language; it doesn't police what one does *with* it—"so theology and doctrine, to the extent that they are second-order activities, assert nothing either true or false about God and his relation to creatures, but only speak *about* such assertions" (*ND*, 69). A grammar *makes explicit* the rules of discourse that were previously implicit in our linguistic "doings." So too theology and doctrine make explicit the commitments implicit in—and entailed by—our proclamation, praise, and prayer.

Inference, Reference, and Truth

None of the above will hearten Christian realists. To the contrary, we need to concede that there are aspects of Lindbeck's proposal that will not sit well with the legions of "objective truth." His notion of doctrine as "second order" seems especially vexing in this regard. For example, as he himself puts it, "for a rule theory . . . doctrines qua doctrines are not first-order propositions, but are to be construed as second-order ones: they make . . . intrasystematic rather than ontological truth claims" (*ND*, 80). Or as he puts it earlier, "Theology and doctrine, to the extent that they are

21. As Lindbeck concedes, this new framing of doctrine doesn't necessarily solve problems of Christian disagreement. However, it does help to locate and crystallize the more fundamental issues that generate such disagreement: "disagreements on where proper grammar is to be found, on who are the competent speakers of a religious language" (*ND*, 113).

22. A cryptic, koan-like fragment in *PI*, §373: "Grammar tells what kind of object anything is. (Theology as grammar.)" I doubt anyone could actually develop whatever "thought" might be here. The notion of theology as grammar is less dependent on this aphorism and more the outworking of the logic of Wittgenstein's account of meaning as use.

second-order activities, assert nothing either true or false about God and his relation to creatures" (69). This almost sounds like a caricature of the sort of irresponsible anti-realism that critics believe is the inevitable consequence of such (Wittgensteinian) positions. To paraphrase Rorty, it would seem that Lindbeck licenses everyone to construct their own religious communities—their own little paradigms, their own little practices, their own little religious language-games—and then crawl into them (see *PM*, 317). In short, it would seem that pragmatism leads to fideism.

But as with the misreading of Rorty on this score, so too critics misread Lindbeck. As we already saw at the end of chapter 3, a pragmatist account of meaning and knowledge does not preclude referential claims; it just accounts for those claims differently—and Brandom further refined just how to make sense of this. In a similar way, there is nothing in Lindbeck's cultural-linguistic account of religion and doctrine that insulates Christian faith from responsibility for "extratextual" claims. Lindbeck is not extolling anti-realism instead of realism; rather, like the pragmatists we have explored, he is ambivalent about the realist/anti-realist binary precisely because both seem locked within a representationalist picture of knowledge—and it is that picture of knowledge that the cultural-linguistic model rejects.[23]

More specifically, Lindbeck's claims about doctrine's "second-order" function need to be read in context. For example, his claim that doctrines "assert nothing either true or false about God" is prefaced by a very important distinction. According to "cognitivist" models, "it is chiefly technical theology and doctrine which are propositional"—which make truth claims and assertions (*ND*, 69). However, the cultural-linguistic model does not *reject* truth claims; it *relocates* them: "On the alternative [cultural-linguistic] model, propositional truth and falsity *characterize ordinary religious language* when it is used to mold lives through prayer, praise, preaching, and exhortation" (69, emphasis added). While doctrine is

---

23. More precisely, Lindbeck puts it this way: "There is nothing in the cultural-linguistic approach that requires the rejection (*or the acceptance*) of the epistemological realism and correspondence theory of truth, which, according to most of the theological tradition, is implicit in the conviction of believers that when they rightly use a sentence such as 'Christ is Lord' they are uttering a true first-order proposition" (*ND*, 68–69, emphasis added). In this respect, Long's proposal for a "realism without representation" but *with* "correspondence" seems quite close to Lindbeck.

"regulative" rather than assertive, such an account of doctrine doesn't *preclude* assertion; it just locates assertion in the lived communal confession of religious practice. Assertion is something we *do*; doctrine regulates our assertions by "conceptualizing" them—articulating the norms implicit in them and thereby allowing us to assess those claims in the "space of reasons." So doctrines articulate the inferential logic that makes our confession coherent. Doctrine is about our claims, not what/Who our claims are about. But such a regulative understanding of doctrine still makes room for—indeed assumes—that those "lived" claims, the assertions we make in praise and prayers, are *about* something. These are our *material* commitments, Brandom would say, and doctrine is the "second-order" attempt to harmonize them as a coherent whole for which we can take epistemic responsibility.

In short, we need to remember that what Lindbeck claims about the limited, "regulative" role of *doctrine* is not a pronouncement about the whole of *religion*. Doctrine is not synonymous with religion, nor is it either the center or foundation of religion. Religion is located primarily in our *doings*, in the practices that constitute a community of worship and devotion to God.[24] In an oft-cited example, Lindbeck considers the claim *Christus est Dominus*, "Christ is Lord." The meaning of the claim—as with any utterance—is bound up with its *use*. This doesn't mean that the meaning is merely utilitarian, as if the claim is true only when it helps us or makes us feel good. Rather, as pragmatism emphasizes, the meaning of the claim is *relative to* a relevant community of practice (in this case, the Christian community; the church) and the "environment" that this community grapples with (which, in this case, includes the revelation of God, the resurrection of Jesus, and the testimony of the apostles).

> Thus for a Christian, "God is Three and One," or "Christ is Lord" are true only as parts of a total pattern of speaking, thinking, feeling, and acting. They are false when their use in any given instance is inconsistent with what the pattern as a whole affirms of God's

24. This emphasis on "doings" has nothing to do with salvation "by works." I use the term in Brandom's sense and only mean that Christian faith is bound up with a *way of life*. That way of life, of course, is a way of life made possible by the unilateral grace of God and the regenerating, empowering work of the Spirit that then makes it possible for us to live a life of discipleship as gratitude for the gift of salvation.

being and will. The crusader's battle cry *"Christus est Dominus,"* for example, is false when used to authorize cleaving the skull of the infidel (even though the same words in other contexts may be a true utterance). When thus employed, it contradicts the Christian understanding of Lordship as embodying, for example, suffering servanthood. (*ND*, 64)

The themes of use, context, and authorization can now be understood within Brandom's framework. The meaning of the claim "Christ is Lord"—like the meaning of *any* assertion—is conditioned by *use*: what the assertion means is *relative to* the context of a particular community of practice. Within a given community of practice, concept users inhabit the "space of reasons" and both give and ask for reasons to justify such assertions. Justification ("authorization") is a *social* phenomenon. And in this case, Lindbeck suggests, the community of practitioners that is the church should not "authorize" the crusader's deployment of these concepts, given the context—a context that includes the community's encounter with the risen Christ, the inheritance of the Scriptures (and the commandments therein), the testimony of the apostles, and the teaching witness of the Christian tradition. This is all part of the obdurate reality with which the church has to "cope," we might say (and with which "the world" must also grapple). Within that community of practice, the crusader's assertion is not "true"—it's not justified or authorized as "rational," given the canons of the ecclesial community of practice. Its falsity and irrationality is a matter of (bad) inferences that cannot be "licensed" by the relevant community of practice.

But again, inference does not preclude reference, but redescribes it. Lindbeck's emphasis on *doctrine*'s second-order, inferential concerns does not preclude assertion. Lindbeck himself is quite clear about this. "If the form of life and understanding of the world shaped by an authentic use of the Christian stories does in fact correspond to God's being and will, then the proper use of *Christus est Dominus* is not only intrasystematically true but also ontologically true" (*ND*, 65). I take it that "ontologically true" is synonymous with what he elsewhere describes as "extratextual" truth. On the one hand, this addresses the realist's worries: the claim that "Jesus is Lord" is a claim *about* the world we inhabit, and is in some sense accountable *to* that environment as part of the context in which "Jesus is Lord" is uttered. On the other hand, this is *not* a back-door representationalism whereby the assertion is true in virtue of simply "mirroring" some reality, independent of a social context. Note the conditions of its truth: it depends upon inculcation into the stories—and the storytelling community—within which "Jesus is Lord" makes *Christian* sense. The "*if*" in that quote above is a recognition of the contingency and contestability of the claim; but recognizing that does not preclude claiming it is *true*. "Their [i.e., the claims] correspondence to reality in the view we are expounding is not an attribute that they have when considered in and of themselves, but is only a function of their role in constituting a form of life, a way of being in the world, which itself corresponds to the Most Important, the Ultimately Real" (*ND*, 65). Part of the scandal of the cross is that the cross cannot be understood for what it is apart from one's being enfolded into the community of practice that confesses "Jesus is Lord." Our knowledge of this reality is relative to, and dependent upon, the Spirit-ed community of practice that is the church. We are dependent upon such a communal context as the condition for understanding this as "the true story of the whole world."

Realism, "Relativism," and Apologetics

This has obvious implications for the church's witness, mission, and proclamation. Indeed, one might worry that a postliberal, pragmatist account of meaning and knowledge would undercut the very possibility of evangelism and outreach. If the truth that "Jesus is Lord" is relative to a particular community of practice, then doesn't that mean the gospel will end up being a secret only known by our little "club," our secret society, our privileged tribe? Doesn't pragmatism thereby result in a kind of postmodern gnosticism, which promises a "secret" available only to the initiated? But isn't the truth of Jesus's resurrection and the proclamation of the good news an inherently *public* truth?

And what possibility is there for apologetics if rationality itself is relative to contingent communities of social practice? What are the prospects for demonstrating the truth of the Christian faith if "logic" is always and only the explicit articulation of the contingent, implicit logic of material inference?

We are right to feel that there are implications here. I don't want to blunt the impact of the pragmatist account as if we could absorb all of this and then just carry on with business as usual. Pragmatism will—*should*—rock our churchly worlds. But it doesn't demolish them; it redescribes and re-orients them. And as I've been arguing, I believe this pragmatist account amounts to a philosophical appreciation of our creaturehood, an appreciation of the contingency that characterizes creatures. So if pragmatism has implications for mission, witness, and apologetics, ultimately I think this amounts to retooling our understanding of mission and evangelism in accord with our creatureliness. This isn't a matter of curtailing missional boldness in order to appease the gods of liberal tolerance; nor is it a matter of trimming our sails to the winds of skepticism. If we need to reframe the tasks of mission, evangelism, and apologetics, this is only because pragmatism is a catalyst to remember the contingency of creaturehood—something we are regularly encouraged to forget in modernity, even (especially) in the modern church.

Once again, Lindbeck was out ahead of us in this regard. Indeed, he anticipated these questions and concerns, granting that "intratextuality seems wholly relativistic: it turns religions, so one can argue, into self-enclosed and incommensurable intellectual ghettoes" (*ND*, 128). In the same ballpark "is the fideistic dilemma: it appears that choice between religions is purely arbitrary, a matter of blind faith" (128). Or, as he puts it more fully a little later, "If there are no universal or foundational structures and standards of judgment by which one can decide between different religious and nonreligious options, the choice of any one of them becomes, it would seem, purely irrational, a matter of arbitrary whim or blind faith" (130). If Christians are going to give up on "Reason" like everyone else, then isn't all lost? That's why, in our pluralist, postmodern context, it would seem even *more* important for Christians to defend the objectivity of reason, champion absolute truth, uphold the standards of a universally knowable natural law, and secure a rational foundation for what we believe.[25] "It seems

25. The foundationalist might pine for the day when "everyone listened to argument," when everyone believed in universal reason and objective truth. The pragmatist has a different account of the same phenomenon: what *seemed* to be a universal rationality is better understood as the success of strategies within a widely shared community of discursive practice that seemed to be synonymous with "everyone." In other words, "classical" or foundationalist apologetic strategies seemed to work

essential in our day," Lindbeck concedes, "to adopt an apologetic approach that seeks to discover a foundational scheme within which religions can be evaluated, and that makes it possible to translate traditional meanings into currently intelligible terms" (*ND*, 129). But of course it is just such foundationalist notions that pragmatism and postliberalism call into question. This would seem to be a "fatal flaw" for the postliberal perspective (129).

What will be jarring to some is the way that Lindbeck aligns the foundationalist project with "liberalism." Liberalism is the "foundationalist enterprise of uncovering universal principles or structures" in order to make Christianity intelligible to nonbelievers (129). While this is "in one sense accommodation to culture" it is nonetheless "often motivated by missionary impulses" (129). We can see this in a Bultmann or a Tillich: the core truth of Christianity is distilled down to and correlated with an "existential" truth that is a universal experience and thus able to be known by all. The truth of the Christian faith is something that can be grasped and appreciated by any lone "rational" individual, and is thus unhooked from any integral relation to the community of practice that is the church. In short, the "recipient" of such apologetic strategies is treated as a lone, atomistic knower capable of independently processing facts and claims against "reality." It's a matter of comparing mirrors. Christian proclamation is thereby "grounded" upon the foundation of a universal reason—but the price to be paid is the distinctiveness of the Christian proclamation, not to mention any recognition of the social conditions of our knowing, the creaturely dependence of knowers upon communities of discursive practice that enable them to make sense of a world.[26] What we end up with are various theisms that are more and more willing to jettison the "irrational" aspects of Christian faith in order to retain a "rational" faith that can be translated into an allegedly "universal" nomenclature.

---

only because of Christendom, an ethos that absorbed such a wide range of practitioners into a particular language-game (even if some might have been rejecting it). "Rationality" here was not universal but widely shared.

26. In other words, the pragmatist account of such foundationalist strategies is always deflationary: it can recognize that such arguments sometimes "work," but they only work *because* knowers have been inducted into inferential logics that emerge from communities of discursive practice. We are all socially dependent knowers, even when we claim to know otherwise.

But we will only appreciate the force of Lindbeck's point if we recognize that this "liberal" strategy is, in fact, widely practiced by "conservative" evangelicals—both those who prize propositional arguments and those who translate the gospel into a "relevant" experience that speaks to the proverbial God-shaped hole that remains in the middle of our consumerist hearts. We either get a rational god who can be known apart from Jesus Christ or a therapeutic god who seems to exist to meet my needs and make me happy. Indeed, the prevalence of "moralistic therapeutic deism" as the gospel that is *effectively* proclaimed and learned in evangelical churches is a testament that even "conservative" strategies that "translate" Christianity into terms that are universally available and comprehensible also lead to the accommodation that Lindbeck warns of. So not only is the foundationalist desire flawed and unattainable, but its effects also seem to undercut the gospel even more than the supposed threat of alleged antifoundationalist tribalism and insularity.

But Lindbeck also refuses to concede that the pragmatist, postliberal model undercuts proclamation and witness. "Postliberals," he emphasizes, are "skeptical, not about missions, but about apologetics and foundations" (*ND*, 129).[27] It's not a question of *whether* we can or ought to engage in mission, but *how*. Our strategies will directly reflect what we think "religion" is, or more specifically, how we understand Christianity. The postliberal project returns to a sense of Christianity as a *form of life*, bound up with the tangible practices of a lived community. It is an inherently *ecclesial* understanding of the gospel whereby the good news of Jesus Christ is now entrusted to—and bound up with—the lived testimony of his body, the church. Foundationalist, apologetic "translation" strategies treat the gospel as an informational set of propositions that can be known by atomistic knowers. But if pragmatism is right (and I think it is), such atomistic, independent knowers don't exist. We bear witness to *human* knowers, contingent social creatures whose knowledge *depends* on the gifts of communities of practice that make the world intelligible. For human knowers, there is no knowledge outside community. Accordingly, there is no knowledge of God in Christ apart from the communal practices of his body, which is home to his Word.

27. It's worth noting that Lindbeck grew up in China as the child of Lutheran missionary parents.

Foundationalist "translation" strategies can, at best, help people acquire a few words from the Christian lexicon; but one learns the *grammar* by immersion. "To the degree that religions are like languages and cultures," Lindbeck summarizes, "they can no more be taught by means of translation than can Chinese or French. What is said in one idiom can to some extent be conveyed in a foreign tongue, but no one learns to understand and speak Chinese by simply hearing and reading translations" (*ND*, 129). One needs to *live* there, be immersed in the community, *absorb* the culture by participating in a way of life. So too "the grammar of religion, like that of language, cannot be explicated or learned by analysis of experience, but only by practice" (129). Postliberalism re-envisions mission and apologetics accordingly.

First, with respect to apologetics, our "defense" of the faith—the task of making Christianity plausible in a post-Christian context—a postliberal approach is ad hoc but not concessionary. Lindbeck is quite clear on this point: the antifoundationalism of the postliberal approach "is not to be equated with irrationalism. The issue is not whether there are universal norms of reasonableness, but whether these can be formulated in some neutral, framework-independent language" (*ND*, 130). This is a crucial point that we have made before: pragmatism's appreciation of the contingent, communal conditions of knowledge does not undercut the ability to make universal claims, nor does it preclude the possibility of asserting universal norms. It only means that it is impossible to see or grasp such norms from "nowhere" or from an "absolute" standpoint. The contingent conditions of a particular community of practice are the *gifts* that enable us to see and understand these "universal" features of the cosmos. But this means that the condition for their being "intelligible" is a degree of competence in the discursive practices of the community (or communities) that see them as such. Instead of undercutting the uniqueness of Christianity, then, this pragmatist account actually heightens it: to see and understand and grasp those "universal" features of God's creation requires the unique capacities bequeathed to us by the community of practice that is the body of Christ. Christian revelation is not less important in this picture, but *more*.[28]

28. Once again, this is also how one could make sense of a Christian pragmatist account of natural law: the Christian affirms that there are "universal" norms inscribed

That doesn't mean there can be no conversation or dialogue across discursive communities. Religious claims "can nevertheless be tested and argued about in various ways, and these tests and arguments in the long run make a difference" (*ND*, 131). Even members of different (ultimate) discursive communities inhabit a shared environment that is a kind of public constraint with which we all grapple. But if knowledge is a *social* accomplishment, and justification is a social effect, then we need to appreciate that "intelligibility comes from skill, not theory, and credibility comes from good performance, not adherence to independently formulated criteria" (131). So "the reasonableness of a religion is largely a function of its assimilative powers, of its ability to provide an intelligible interpretation in its own terms of the varied situations and realities adherents [and nonadherents] encounter" (131). In other words, the apologetic strategy of Christian pragmatism (i.e., postliberalism) is quite similar to that of Plantinga's Reformed epistemology: we engage ad hoc strategies to level the playing field and retain space for Christianity's plausibility in postmodernity, but ultimately Christian faith is not something that can be proven or demonstrated. Instead, in the shared space of public debate, the proverbial "marketplace of ideas," we continue to bear witness to the truth of the gospel (and not just "theism"), making ad hoc cases that push back on challengers and seek to "warrant" a Christian account of the world. This clears space to invite nonbelievers to consider the specifics of the Christian story. We can invite them to "try on" Christian faith as a way to make sense of the cosmos and their place in it. They can "try out" Christianity's "assimilative powers": "Consider the Christian story," we suggest to our neighbor. "Tell me if this helps makes sense of your world of experience. Here's a Christian account of who we are and whose we are and where we've come from and what we might hope for, all bound up with the story of God in Christ reconciling the world to himself. Does that do a *better* job of making sense of the world than the other accounts you've 'tried on'?" That is the shape of a postliberal apologetic strategy: it is a

---

into the very structure of creation. We might describe this as an "ontological" claim. However, the epistemic condition for *seeing* them—the condition of their "intelligibility"—is immersion in the Spirit-ed community of practice that receives the Word of God. I take this as a way to understand the noetic effects of sin in Romans 1:18–31.

wager of outnarration.[29] "This process certainly does not enable individuals to decide between major alternatives on the basis of reason alone," Lindbeck admits. "But it does provide warrants for taking reasonableness in religion seriously."[30]

It also explains why a postliberal model of apologetics is inextricably linked to a postliberal model of evangelism. The only point of postliberal apologetics is to make Christianity just plausible enough that a nonbeliever might actually *try on a way of life* found in the body of Christ, because ultimately Christian faith is a know-*how* absorbed in a community of practice and can never be reduced to propositional content. So postliberal apologetics is invitational, not demonstrational. Rooted in the conviction that Christianity is more like a culture than an intellectual system, postliberal evangelism is effectively an invitation to immigrate to a different world, to become citizens of a different culture through immersion in the practices of the people of God. Lindbeck recognizes that this "is bound to be unpopular among those chiefly concerned to maintain or increase the membership and influence of the church" (*ND*, 132). This is because postliberal evangelism

> resembles ancient catechesis more than modern translation. Instead of redescribing the faith in new concepts, it seeks to teach the language and practices of the religion to potential adherents. This has been the primary way of transmitting the faith and winning converts for most religions down through the centuries. In the early days of the Christian church, for example, it was the gnostics, not the catholics, who were most inclined to redescribe biblical materials in a new interpretive framework. Pagan converts to the catholic mainstream did not, for the most part, first understand the faith and then decide to become Christians; rather, the process was reversed: they first decided and then they understood. More precisely, they were first attracted by the Christian community and form of life. (*ND*, 132)

The ancient catechumenate is here invoked as the ideal mode of postmodern evangelism. Ancient resources are retrieved as wise

29. Again, I think this is analogous to Charles Taylor's "best account" (BA) strategy in *Sources of the Self*.

30. *ND*, 131. Again, compare this strategy with the shape of Alvin Plantinga's "Reformed" apologetic in *Warranted Christian Belief* (New York: Oxford University Press, 2000).

resources for the church's future. We might be familiar with this logic as "belonging before believing." But this is not just a matter of belonging to a friendly club, as if the church were *Cheers*—just a place where everybody knows your name. No, this was more like belonging to a "people," a nation marked by overarching narratives enacted and embodied in concrete practices that shape our communal perception of the world. Evangelism is not just about convincing people to believe but rather inculcating them into a form of life, into a community of practice organized around a "final story."

Rather than translating the peculiar transcendence of the church's practices into some allegedly "neutral" vernacular, we bear witness to God in Christ by enfolding nonadherents into a communal way of life, with all of its rhythms and rituals. In short, historic liturgy becomes our evangelistic strategy—not because this is "traditional," but because the implicit know-*how* fostered by these practices is rooted in the canonical Scriptures that bear witness to the risen, returning Christ. Because we are called to make not just "believers" but *disciples*, we do well to consider the ancient catechumenate—which might even look positively inhospitable to our modern penchant for translation—as a paradigm for postmodern proclamation. When we look back at ancient catechumens, we'll see that "they submitted themselves to prolonged catechetical instruction in which they practiced new modes of behavior and learned the stories of Israel and their fulfillment in Christ. Only after they had acquired proficiency in the alien Christian language and the form of life were they deemed able intelligently and responsibly to profess the faith, to be baptized" (*ND*, 132).

This vision, however, should also give us pause—not because it is not "realist" or foundationalist or rational, but precisely because it assumes that there *is* such a community of practice into which nonbelievers might be invited. In our current context, this is increasingly becoming a minority report as much of North American Christianity has translated itself into eviscerated "relevant" communities that bear little if any resemblance to the communities of practice Lindbeck envisions. Indeed, he already anticipated this: given the dominance of experiential-expressive "translation," fewer and fewer churches sustain the practices necessary to be such an *attractive*, formative community of Christian practice. This is an evangelistic strategy *if and only if* there are communities of "thick"

Christian practice that preserve this "culture." One could worry that we might have already passed a tipping point in this respect: "The conditions for practice seem to be steadily weakening. Disarray in church and society makes the transmission of the necessary skills more and more difficult" (ND, 124).

If that is true, then in fact the condition for evangelism will be the renewal of Christian communities of practice. "When or if dechristianization reduces Christians to a small minority," Lindbeck counsels, "they will need for the sake of survival to form communities that strive without traditionalist rigidity to cultivate their native tongue and learn to act accordingly" (ND, 134). That time has arrived. We need to tend to the practices of the church if there is going to be a community that can bear witness to the gospel.

In this respect, I'm reminded of a script I have heard a hundred times, often only vaguely in the background after the airplane door closes and I'm powering down my iPhone. It's a bit of information you hope you'll never need, and so you listen with some detachment to the flight attendant's instructions.

> Oxygen and the air pressure are always being monitored. In the event of a decompression, an oxygen mask will automatically appear in front of you. To start the flow of oxygen, pull the mask toward you. Place it firmly over your nose and mouth, secure the elastic band behind your head, and breathe normally. Although the bag does not inflate, oxygen is flowing to the mask. If you are traveling with a child or someone who requires assistance, secure your mask first, and then assist the other person. Keep your mask on until a uniformed crew member advises you to remove it.

If you're traveling with someone who requires assistance, they admonish, take care of yourself first. This might sound like selfishness, but of course it is really about being equipped to assist the other. I can't help my neighbor breathe if I'm gasping for air; I can't help others with their mask if I've failed to attend to my own situation first. I think this might be a helpful metaphor to help us picture the urgency of the church's situation in postmodernity. With perhaps the best of missionary intentions, we have spent a generation trying to help others put on their air mask, but never attended to our own. In our outward-oriented zeal to translate the faith into "relevant" messages for a post-Christian culture, we have only eviscerated the community of *practice* necessary to sustain witness to the risen Christ. In this respect, Lindbeck's exhortation might seem counterintuitive: mission *to* and *for* the world depends upon the church being the church, attending to the practices passed down to us by the tradition.

> The general point is that, provided a religion stresses service rather than domination, it is likely to contribute more to the future of humanity if it preserves its own distinctiveness and integrity than if it yields to the homogenizing tendencies associated with liberal experiential-expressivism. The conclusion is paradoxical: Religious communities are likely to be practically relevant in the long run to the degree that they do not first ask what is either practical or relevant, but instead concentrate on their own intratextual outlooks and forms of life. (*ND*, 128)

To invite the world to see itself otherwise—to see itself in light of Christ, in whom all things hold together (Col. 1:17)—we need to foster communities of practice where that is possible. Only if *we* practice the faith will we be able to invite others into a form of life in which they might learn what it means to "use" the world as the creation of a gracious God who loves us and gave himself for us.

Epilogue

How to Be a Conservative Relativist

"Relativism" can mean many different things. We usually trot out the word as an epithet that is synonymous with anything-goes nihilism. But in doing so, I have tried to show, we use the word in a very sloppy, imprecise way. We confuse something's being "relative" with being *arbitrary* or *subjective* or governed only by fleeting whims.

So my first goal was to introduce some philosophical precision about how we use the term "relativism" (a good *analytic* project!). I am trying to return the term to its more obvious meaning: "relativism" would describe claims or accounts that are, well, *relative*—*related to* something or Someone, relative to, say, a context or a community. As relative *to*, what's "relative" is *dependent upon*—is contingent. A claim, a principle, a view is *relative* just to the extent that "*it depends*." That is very different from saying that something is arbitrary and free-floating and dependent on nothing. Indeed, relativism would be almost the exact opposite; the "relativist" emphasizes, with William Carlos Williams, that "so much depends" not just on red wheelbarrows but on all the vagaries and contingencies that are part and parcel of our creaturehood—especially the networks of social relationships that weave our identities and our ultimate dependence upon the Creator himself, who is truly known and revealed and related to in Christ. So rather than misusing the word "relativism" to mean *nothing matters*, I'm arguing that relativism means *everything depends*—and that such a claim is a radically creational, radically Christian claim about the status of creaturehood, including creaturely knowing.

So, as I have been pointing out, the condition of "being relative"—being dependent, being contingent—is also synonymous with the conditions of creaturehood. Only the Creator is necessary, independent, and absolute in himself. But we're not God (always good to be reminded of that!). And that Absolute Being has bound himself covenantally to a people; otherwise we could never know him. The incarnation is the Absolute's refusal to remain absolved of relation to humanity. As creatures, we are contingent, dependent, and relative (i.e., in relation—to the Creator, but also to other creatures). Relativism, then, in this more precise sense, is just a name for the human condition, the *ethos* of creaturehood.

This is why it borders on idolatrous *hubris* for humans to claim *absolute* truth (i.e., truth ab-solved of relation, truth that is *in*-dependent) as their defense against "relativism" (by which they mean anything-goes-ism). We ought to reject anything-goes-ism, of course. But the alternative to anything-goes-ism is *not* some absolute standpoint. Just because we want to avoid arbitrariness doesn't mean we can excuse ourselves from contingency; just because we eschew nihilism doesn't mean we get to avail ourselves of necessity. To do so would be to imagine we can somehow transcend the conditions of creaturehood—which is usually considered diabolical, the root of all transgression. To pretend to the Absolute is the act that leads to the fall.

Instead, we creatures are called to depend rightly—*relate* rightly—to the One who is Absolute but graciously condescends to our finitude in the incarnation. In Jesus—the Absolute becomes dependent, Necessity inhabiting contingency—we learn *how* to be dependent. And as contingent *rational* creatures, we are called into rightly ordered communities of discursive practice.

A number of strategies we often employ to ward off anything-goes-ism are actually expressions of a desire to overcome our finitude, deny our dependence, and somehow efface the contingency of creaturehood. Our attempts to establish "foundations" and secure "absolute" truth are tantamount to attempts to achieve a standpoint that is God-like rather than being related *to* God. This is why, following Richard Rorty, I have tried to introduce pragmatism as a kind of *therapeutic* philosophy—a critical, "deflationary" philosophical tradition that punctures the balloons of our pretensions even as it topples the epistemological Babels of our own making, testaments of our attempts to claim heaven and achieve a God's-eye view. Pragmatism is a resource and ally for Christian philosophy precisely because it is a philosophy of contingency, ruthlessly attentive to our dependence and sociality. In the spirit of Augustine's "looting of the Egyptians," much of pragmatism's account of meaning, truth, and knowledge can be appropriated as a philosophy of creaturehood—even though this obviously requires resisting the direction in which particular pragmatists like Rorty and Brandom *ultimately* go. The selective appropriation of their insights is part of the discernment that has always characterized critical Christian engagement with our philosophical neighbors, from St. Paul through St. Augustine and St. Thomas, up to John Calvin and Jonathan Edwards. There is no "package deal" that has to be purchased. We are free to selectively appropriate the insights of pragmatism just insofar as they help us to understand facets of God's creation and our own creaturehood.

Now such a project—a Christian pragmatism, even a "Christian relativism"—might seem like a "progressive" agenda. But, in fact, the conditions of dependence and social contingency recognized and analyzed by pragmatism are the same conditions that undergird a classical, "Burkean" conservatism that recognizes and appreciates the *debts* we owe simply by virtue of being human—that we are gifted by communities that precede us and surround us, and that we are heirs of legacies that make possible even our critique.

Conversely, the "atomistic" epistemology that is bound up with representationalist realism is actually liberal and subjectivist. It posits a picture of the lone, self-sufficient knower able to "mirror" the world without help, independently. Thus Charles Taylor notes that the Cartesian turn unleashes a subjectivism that has ripple effects across culture. "Now [after Descartes] certainty is something the mind has to generate for itself. It requires a reflexive turn, where instead of simply trusting the opinions you have acquired through your upbringing, you examine their foundation, which is ultimately to be found in your own mind."[1] I, the subject, am put

---

1. Charles Taylor, "Overcoming Epistemology," in *Philosophical Arguments* (Cambridge, MA: Harvard University Press, 1995), 5.

in the place of arbitrator and judge, throwing off the taint of external influences.[2] This is why "absolute" truth is liberal: it denies dependence and denies any indebtedness of knowers to tradition.

How odd, then, that we somehow reached the default position that a Christian account of knowledge should be a representationalist epistemology! The picture of knowledge and knowers that is bound up with this paradigm seems more like self-idolatry than faithful knowing. This is why I see pragmatism as a philosophical catalyst for Christians to recover both a more biblical appreciation for contingency and dependence and—because of that—a fundamentally *catholic* stance that begins with an affirmation of tradition, a gracious reception of the gifts we receive from our past.

I recognize that this is not the usual trajectory that pragmatism takes. Indeed, Rorty is very much a "progressive." But I would suggest that in fact pragmatism is ambivalent and underdetermined on this score. And that the gravity of pragmatism's insights about contingency and dependence are more *properly* expressed in a kind of "conservatism." Indeed, even Rorty recognizes the "antidemocratic implications" of a Hegelian insight that he fundamentally affirms: "that the individual apart from society is just one more animal" (*PM*, 192).[3] Or consider, for example, the curious invocation of Michael Oakeshott in the last part of *Philosophy and the Mirror of Nature*, including the final exhortation to "continue the conversation of the West" (*PM*, 264, 318, 389). If pragmatism is a philosophical account of our contingency, dependence, and social indebtedness, then "conservatism" might be its best expression insofar as conservatism (not to be confused with the libertarian cynicism that sometimes takes on the name) is a stance and orientation that is rooted above all in gratitude. Critical of those "revolutionary" proposals that spurn the gifts of the tradition and pretend to be ahistorical and independent, pragmatist insights about contingency and solidarity could even be described as *catholic*.

2. This all comes to fruition in Kant's "What Is Enlightenment?," in which the rational subject is the one who has thrown off all tradition, all authority, and certainly all religious influence.

3. This is the same Hegel, the Hegel of the *Elements of the Philosophy of Right*, that so influences Brandom's expressivist account of rationality.

Author Index

183

Subject Index

Printed in Great Britain
by Amazon